SKIPNESS:
Memories of a Highland Estate

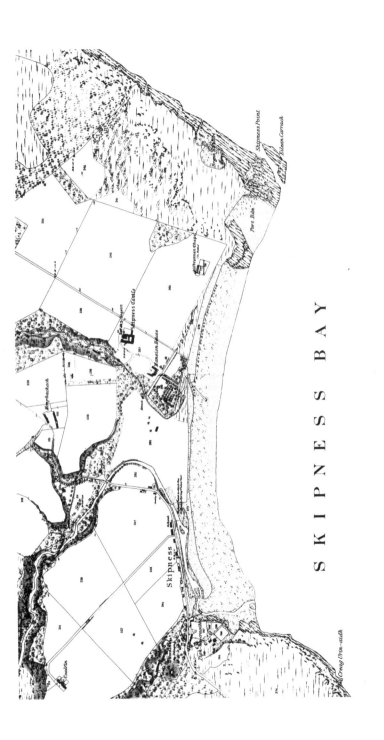

Detail of Ordnance Survey map of 1867, showing Skipness Old House.

SKIPNESS BAY

Skipness

Angus Graham

SKIPNESS:
Memories of a Highland Estate

Birlinn

This edition published in 2005
by Birlinn Limited
West Newington House
10 Newington Road
Edinburgh
EH9 1QS

www.birlinn.co.uk

First published in 1993 by
Canongate Academic, Edinburgh

British Library Cataloguing in Publication Data
A catalogue record for ths book is available from
the British Library

ISBN10: 1 84158 420 7
ISBN13: 978 1 84158 1 420 1

Facsimile origination by Brinnoven, Livingston
Printed and bound by Antony Rowe, Chippenham

Contents

GENIO LOCI
VETERVMQUE
MANIBUS
AG
VSLLM

Acknowledgements

Professor Alexander Fenton first encouraged me to publish Angus Graham's book about Skipness. The staff of the Map Room of the National Library of Scotland have extended to me the invaluable experience they have always given the author. Much kind help has been given by the Oakes family, Mr and Mrs G.E.S. Dunlop and by the other residents of Skipness today. The work of editing has been a co-operative effort by my uncle's family, friends and colleagues, to all of whom I am most grateful. Thanks go to Vera Collingwood for preparing photographs and thanks also go to Pamela Rachet for providing the drawings. The 1867 and 1899 Ordnance Survey maps on pages ii and 142 are reproduced by permission of the Trustees of the National Library of Scotland, and plates 3 and 4 by permission of the Royal Commission on the Ancient and Historical Monuments of Scotland, who hold the copyright.

Joanna Gordon

Skipness: location map.

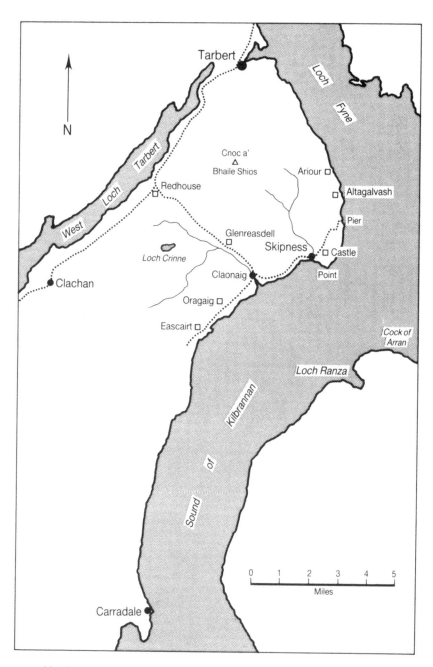

Northern Kintyre, showing some of the farms mentioned in Chapter 17.

Foreword

Angus Graham was born in 1892 in the remarkable house, almost a fairytale castle, with which the Grahams replaced, in 1881, the eighteenth-century mansion of the former Campbells of Skipness. Some sympathy may be felt for the architect, John Honeyman, as Italianate and pre-Raphaelite decorations contributed by the family softened the baronial impact. His father, Robert Chellas Graham, had met his English mother, Emily Eliza Hardcastle, in Rome in 1875. Emily, and Robert's widowed Anglo-Dutch mother, born Susan Roope Schuyler, both kept diaries of those fashionable artistic winters abroad so characteristic of their class and times. Equally characteristic aspirations to land ownership led Robert's mother to purchase for him the estate of Skipness.

Angus, the youngest of Emily's two sons and three daughters, remembered being 'entered to archaeology at the age of six'. His father had been officially ordered to demolish the medieval castle of Skipness, as a dangerous structure, but was allowed to renovate it at his own expense after carrying out a rescue excavation.

Isolated at Skipness, R. C. Graham depended upon membership of learned societies for all of his intellectual life, hence an acquaintance with Joseph Anderson, Director of the National Museum of Antiquities of Scotland, of whose work Angus published a study in the *Proceedings of the Society of Antiquaries of Scotland* (No. 107). The Grahams, father and son, responded consistently to Anderson's demand, in his Rhind Lectures of 1879, for 'systematic and precise examination of the objects themselves as the basis for scientific archaeology'. Angus wrote of his own work on pre-1855 harbours, 'It is an archaeological exercise, and historical matter is introduced only so far as it serves to explain the structures'. Although so different from today's interdisciplinary approach, this pure Anderson doctrine served Angus well, as it had served his father in writing his careful and lavishly illustrated inventory of 'The Carved Stones of Islay'. Angus got his name from the last word his father wrote before being interrupted with the news from upstairs of his second son's birth.

The outdoor life of Skipness, along the shore, in boats, and up the hill probably enabled Angus to survive later campaigns, at Gallipoli and in Palestine, as a forester in Canada, and in field archaeology up to his 87th year, though he was born asthmatic and nearly died of pneumonia at Winchester. He respected his prep-school, Sandroyd, for having taught him all the arithmetic he ever knew, or needed, and Winchester as a forcing ground so specialised in Greek and Latin literature that English was not on the curriculum. He prepared for the Oxford School of Litterae Humaniores with coaching at Skipness by one of the Edinburgh Lorimers, and a summer in Germany to learn the language of the best contemporary classical scholars. Feeling rather better, he enjoyed Germany, the beer, the opera, and the nightingales in the Berlin Tiergarten.

At New College, Oxford, of which he always remained a loyal alumnus, he never conformed to current intellectual convention. He chose Homeric Archaeology as his special subject, 'for relief from everlasting speeches, poetry and plays'. Professor Sir John Myers re-introduced him to archaeology. His first excavation was of Dun Breac (see page 26) and he made his own first inventory, listing the ancient remains in Skipness Parish (*Proceedings of the Society of Antiquaries of Scotland* 1918-20). From such archaeological work he saw his later career in forestry as no more than a long diversion, financially necessary for him as the younger son.

Even the war of 1914-18 failed to divert Angus from

archaeology, though it finally ruined his health. Iller than ever internally, after Gallipoli, he was also wounded, and carried lead shot in the spine to his grave.

Convalescing in Egypt and Malta, Angus was found in museums and on excavation sites whenever physically strong enough to extricate himself from hospitals. The Blue Nuns in Malta were not very strict, and constant companionship with horses, as a Staff Officer of the Highland Light Infantry, had at least cured his asthma. Thereafter, Angus chose forestry, intending to combine it with archaeological pursuits. Professor Sir William Schlich admitted him to the Diploma Course at Oxford, remarking that anyone who read Greats showed he could master the science of forest botany if he wished. His tutor, H.E. Hiley, advised him to apply for the post of Scientific Adviser to the firm of Price Bros., Quebec, after brief service with the Forestry Commission in Argyll, from which Angus was axed by Geddes. Price Bros. stationed him at Rimouski for easy access to their woods. Specialising later in legal and administrative questions relating to Quebec, he wrote a book, *The Quebec Limit Holders' Manual*, for the Quebec Forest Industries Association. He knew, he said, 'a great deal about stealing timber'. For his work, and his own inclination, he mastered the geology and history of the forest areas of Canada, having already studied those of France and Sweden, besides Argyll. His Canadian diary is full of bears, moose, beavers, and their hunters and trappers, and he recorded the numerous races of sparrows. In Argyll, he had seen that pre-existent plant communities were good indicators of the suitability of planting areas for specific trees. With his friend W. G. Wright, he combined this observation with the now common idea that fire does not always interrupt, but is normally pivotal to the long cycle of change in the composition of natural forests.

Among many descendants of earlier Scottish immigrants, Price Bros.' head woodsman had a Scottish name and a West Highland face, although he spoke only French and was illiterate. Angus learned Canadian French from such foresters, habitant settlers, priests, officials and politicians, and never lost the accent. He enjoyed the social life which centred on the Quebec Garrison Club. His tailor visited Quebec annually from London and made suits some of which he wore to the end of his life. Canadian life provided subjects for stories in *Blackwood's Magazine*, and a later novel *Napoleon Tremblay*. Angus always wanted to be a writer of fiction, but his best-selling book is an account of the experience of an older Canadian friend, James Mitchell, injured on a dreadful goldrush journey and rescued by Indians, who mended his fractured knee as they would one of their own. The highly readable *Golden Grindstone* was followed, characteristically, by a short factual article which Angus published in *Antiquity*, entitled 'Surgery with Flint'.

Angus left Canada in 1933, and came to London, too ill to fight the conditions prevailing in the timber industry at the height of the Depression. By modern standards, his time of insecurity and job-hunting was not long, particularly for a sick man in his forties, for by the summer of 1935 he was Secretary of the Royal Commission on the Ancient Monuments of Scotland. He had undergone drastic medical treatment and completed and published *The Golden Grindstone* before returning to Scotland, and the full-time archaeology which occupied the forefront of his mind for the rest of his life. Though not then, or ever, fully cured of dysentery, he took only temporary lodgings in Edinburgh and hastened to Shetland until fieldwork closed for the winter. Eventually, he bought a first-floor flat in No 1 Nelson Street, looking south over Queen Street Gardens. He usually walked to the Commission's offices, or through the Gardens to the Queen Street Museum. In the Royal Botanic Gardens he made an early observation of the arrival in those latitudes of the collared dove. He said his housekeepers probably stayed so long because they liked opening the enormous front door to 'a very good class of visitor'.

His contribution to the Bi-Centenary volume of the Society of Antiquaries of Scotland, of which he was Secretary for many years, is an account of his more notable associates, restrained by a fastidious reluctance to publicise the mildest criticism. Even so, it was obviously written with some wry smiles. He was routinely publishing articles in learned journals at the same time as producing the Commission's Inventories for Roxburgh, Selkirk, Peebles and Stirlingshire. His very high standards as an editor are well remembered. The Kintyre volume of the Argyll Inventory was published after his retirement, but drew on his knowledge. Archaeologists found him open to new ideas, though not himself an innovator. By contrast, his very advanced views on the role of fire in forests had been anathema to his Canadian employers, whose business was to insure against it, while plant communities have only recently become a commonplace of botany. Perhaps Angus worked his mind differently in Canada, when he was young and thinking tangentially to his lifelong vocation.

All I can add is a tribute to Angus as a particularly delightful and helpful uncle to both his nephews, all four nieces and their families, almost all of whom were present when his ashes were interred at Skipness, on a perfect day in July 1980.

Joanna Gordon

Author's Preface

I was born at Skipness in 1892, lived there as a boy, went back as occasion offered in later years, and maintained a close connection with the place until 1922, when I went abroad. As a result, I can either remember from my own experience, or have been told by my elders or have otherwise come to know, a good deal about what went on there in the later nineteenth century, and am now being pressed by friends to write down my reminiscences for record. Reminiscences, however, will hardly stand up by themselves, and I have therefore tried to underpin them with a general description of the ground, and by historical inference based on the few available facts.

In the task of recalling and recording I have been helped in a variety of ways by Mrs Collingwood, the late Dr James Coutts, Mr J.G. Dunbar, Mr G.E.S. Dunlop, Miss J. Gordon, Mrs R.F. Graham, Professor K.H. Jackson, Mr A. Maclaren, Sir Owen and Lady O'Malley and Miss G.E. Vaughan Johnson. I have obtained much fresh information from the Ancient Monuments Commission's *Inventory of Kintyre*; and have also been able, through the kindness of the late Hon. Mrs Scott of Harden, to consult the diaries of the late Mrs Robert Campbell of Skipness, which began in 1807. A good deal of local folklore, as well as some facts, was preserved by the late Mrs Higginson, a former resident, in a manuscript collection of stories held by the School of Scottish Studies, University of Edinburgh. The maps referred to from time to time are as follows: Ordnance Survey six-inch map of Argyll, surveyed in 1867, sheets CCII, CCXIII; do. one-inch map of Great Britain, 7th series, sheet 58; Roy's map of Scotland (1747-55),

photostat in the National Library of Scotland; Taylor, G. and
Skinner, A., *Survey and Maps of the Roads of . . . Scotland*
(1776), Pl.17; George Langlands and Son, map of Argyllshire
(1801); Thomson's Atlas (1824), No.17. Six-figure references
to the National Grid are all to 100km square NR.

Detailed map references are to be found in *The Early Maps
of Scotland*, Royal Scottish Geographical Society, Vol. 1 to
1775, Vol. 2 to 1850, Edinburgh 1973. Further references are:
William Dobie, Perambulations in Kintyre. 1833. MS 573,
Library of the Society of Antiquaries of Scotland; Shore, C.J.,
2nd Lord Teignmouth, *Sketches of the Coasts and Islands of
Scotland and the Isle of Man*, 2 vols., 1836; and White, Capt.
T.P., *Archaeological Sketches in Scotland. Kintyre*, 1873.

The estate had been in Campbell hands since 1511, when
it was given to Archibald, second son of the second Earl
of Argyll. Subsequent Campbell lairds were his son Jon
(1537); Walter Campbell of Ardkinglass, who had married
Jane, daughter of the second laird (after 1563); their son
Matthew (1614-1618); his son Angus (c.1702); his son Colin;
his nephew John (1756), grandson of Daniel Campbell of
Shawfield, himself eldest son of Walter, fifth of Skipness;
his brother Walter, of Islay; his son Robert, to whom he
gave the estate on his marriage in 1807; his son Walter
(1814). The last-named sold the estate in 1843 to William
Fraser, whose son sold it in 1866 to trustees for my father,
then eighteen years old, my grandfather, Robert Graham of
Brooksby, having died in 1854. The leading member of the
trust was my grandmother, Susan Roope Schuyler, daughter
of Captain Adoniah Schuyler, RN; she was largely responsible
for the campaign of estate improvement that now began. The
estate came to my brother on the death of my mother in 1933,
and he sold it to the late Mr C.A.M. Oakes in 1936.

1. GENERAL VIEW

Skipness can be placed by adapting some words of one of the Fathers of History, Thucydides, and exchanging his starboard for port. That is to say, it is a village on the left for anyone who sails into Loch Fyne from Kilbrannan Sound, the Sound itself being a strip of water, from three to six miles wide, which separates the peninsula of Kintyre from the island of Arran. Beyond Skipness Point the wide mouth of Loch Fyne opens towards the north, while eastwards, towards Inch Marnock, Bute and the north end of Arran, the Sound of Bute gives access to the Firth of Clyde. Skipness Bay is a stretch of white, shingly beach, running from west to east and just a mile in length; behind this stand the village, the policy woods, the walled and wooded garden of the House, the Castle, with its high wall of enceinte and a tower-house rising in one corner, and the roofless Chapel conspicuous in a large green field. In the east the Bay ends at the Point, which at high tide takes the form of a blunt spur rather than of a projection, and marks an abrupt change in the alignment of the coast; but as the tide goes down a ridge of rocks appears, running out south-south-west, and this, with an extension under water which is never uncovered, pushes out the five-fathom line to something like a third of a mile. To turn the Point safely when entering the bay from Loch Fyne, the seaman's rule was to hold a southerly course until the road from the village to the high-standing farm of Caolfin was pointing straight up and down.

The Point calls for a particular word of notice, as it has generated the place-name Skipness. This represents the Norse

Skipanes, 'ship-point'. It is true that the name is, or was, locally pronounced 'Shkeepenish', Gaelic Sgiobanis, and that forms ending in '-nish' or '-inch' (Schepehinche, Skipinche, Skippeneische, etc.) are used in mediaeval and later charters; but Professor W.F.H. Nicolaisen, to whom I am indebted for my information on this subject, assures me that these forms could well have been derived from Sgiobanis, the trend towards '-inch' (island or flat meadow) perhaps being helped by a kind of popular etymology.

On his way up the Sound towards Skipness, the incomer's way is flanked, on the port hand, by a landscape which is mildly romantic but unspectacular by accepted West Highland standards. Kintyre is some forty miles long and from five to eight miles wide, and has for its spine an irregular ridge of heathery and peaty hills none of which is more than fifteen hundred feet high. The east coast, south of Skipness, carries small whitewashed farms with their fields strung out rather thinly along the lower slopes; cultivable soil is rare at more than three hundred feet above the sea, while the lowermost ground of all is generally uncultivable too, as it tends to consist of rocks, low cliffs, and gullies overgrown with scrubwoods of oak, birch and hazel. Only in the mouths of the burns, and in the wider bays, do gussets of green pasture emerge and run down to beaches of sand. North of the Point even these concessions are soon withdrawn, much of the coast that fronts on Loch Fyne being impossibly steep and rock-bound, with the scrub stretching up in places to three or four hundred feet. The shore forms part of a Site of Special Scientific Interest reaching beyond Skipness all the way to Tarbert.

Skipness itself as a habitable place owes its existence to its geological formation. The troughs now flooded by Loch Fyne and the Kilbrannan Sound follow fault lines. When the glaciers which moved along these openings melted, and the land rose as the raised beaches show, a ridge of five hundred million-year-old hard rock, visible today at Skipness Point, protected the small triangle of land lying behind the Bay, leaving enough of it to clear the later encroachments of the sea and ultimately to provide a site for men to live on. The base of this triangle is the Bay, and its apex lies a mile towards the north-north-east, close to the farm of Culindrach; no part of it stands as much as two hundred feet above the sea, while the slopes are gentle and much of the surface is farmland. And whereas the sea, standing at higher levels in Raised Beach times, cut out a belt of gullies, pinnacles and cliffs where the coast was rocky, when it came to act on the boulder-clay and gravels behind the Bay it smoothed out a series of easy, south-facing terraces which must always have invited cultivation.

So much for the Kintyre side of the frame in which Skipness is set, but something must be said about the Arran side as well, as Skipness cannot be thought of in separation from its view southwards to Arran. That island took shape after the formation of the hard rock of Skipness Point (and long before the final melting of the ice), when volcanoes erupted along a moving line of strain in the earth's crust which reached and passed this latitude before progressing northwards as far as the volcanic field of Iceland today. The north end of Arran is a tremendous blob of granite, split up into a tangle of mountains, corries and glens. The highest mountain, Goat Fell, of 2866ft, is barely visible from Skipness, and can only be picked out from among the other peaks by someone who knows what to look for; but Caisteal Abhail, which is only about fifty feet lower, stands squarely in the middle of the prospect, with a vast corrie in front of its gently arching summit-ridge and a sierra of lower or more distant peaks to the left. The base of this great massif is framed by a wide V of nearer hills, which rise directly from the sea to heights of from a thousand to eighteen hundred feet, the centre of the V being the small inlet of Loch Ranza; these lower ranges end, on the left, in a long, even slope running down to Millstone Point, while their western faces, between Catacol and Whitefarland Point, gradually fall away and foreshorten. The island is capable of assuming any shade of blue, mauve or purple, and someone who caught it in a certain kind of sunset once painted it a strong rose-pink. In the middle of winter the sun rises only just clear of Millstone

Point, and then, as its path is flatter than the slope above the Point, it shortly sets again, sideways, behind the hillside, to make a second and permanent appearance some time later from the surface of the plateau above. Caisteal Abhail and the peaks to the east of it can be seen as forming the silhouette of a 'Sleeping Warrior'. One peak makes the visor of his helmet, and the next two his nose and chin; a hollow provides for his neck, while the summit-ridge itself rises up to a generous belly with appropriate knobs for buttons.

A picture of the Skipness hinterland can best be obtained by considering the course and surroundings of a large burn, which drains much of the northern part of the estate and discharges into the Bay. An anomaly seems to attach to the name of this burn, as well as to those of other local streams. The Ordance Survey marks it as the 'Skipness River', but no such name was ever heard in the mouths of the people, who alluded to it simply as 'the burn', or 'the big burn' if further identification was called for. It is true that the glen through which it runs is called 'Glen Skibble', and that this name is at least as old as 1495, but this does not advance the subject as the name applies only to the glen, not to the burn, and in any case seems to be derived from a Norse word 'Skipdalr', which goes back to the 'Skio' of Skipness. (I am indebted for this information to Professor W.F.H. Nicolaisen). The same thing happens in the case of the Ordnance Survey's 'Claonaig Water', the next large burn to the south, which is again simply 'the burn' to the people living at Claonaig; while other burns seem now generally to be called after neighbouring farms of lochs.

The 'Skipness River', then, runs approximately from north to south, having two headwater branches, each about two miles long, which unite at a point about two miles inland from the village. The ground adjoining these headwaters is rough and inhospitable, and rises, at about a thousand feet above the sea, to the watershed between Loch Fyne and West Loch Tarbert. This is a region of remarkably sinister aspect, as it carries, instead of the ordinary blanket-peat of the lower

levels, thick beds of fine, black peat formed in a climate quite
different from that of today, and now weathering down to the
ancient surface of the land. At the bottom there are roots of
trees overwhelmed by the peat as it grew, some of them still
bearing the silvery bark of the birch. Shallow ponds appear
here and there, with cotton-grass showing white tufts in and
among them, and two larger lochs. Loch na Machrach Moire
is in fact the source of the eastern branch of the burn, but Loch
na Machrach Rige is just outside the burn's drainage-basin,
and its discharge runs down north-eastwards to the coast
of Loch Fyne, distant rather more than a mile. Much of
the ground lying east of the basin is again high and bleak,
though improving at lower levels and in the region nearer
Skipness.

The western branch rises on the flank of Cnoc a' Bhaile
Shios, the highest hill in the northern part of Kintyre. Though
no more than 1383ft high, this place manages to seem like the
top of a real mountain – the surroundings are as desolate
as the peat-hags of Loch na Machrach, the summit itself
is rock scourged bare by the elements, and the nearer hills
are so placed as to permit an unexpectedly wide view. One
sees at once what the Psalmist had in mind when saying that
Moab was his wash-pot, as West Loch Tarbert lies below in
exactly that humble character; but there the parallel stops, for
no-one could cast out his shoe over the Paps of Jura, which
rise in the west to double the height of Cnoc a' Bhaile Shios.
Southwards Rathlin is plain, with the mountains of Antrim
beyond, and northwards the unmistakable summits of Ben
Cruachan.

The two branches join up near the ruined houses of
Glenskibble, where the land in the angle once supported
cultivation. Below the forks the valley deepens and narrows,
receiving no further tributary of any significance, and gradually
becomes dominated by high, red-clay scars. Where the clay
is not bare and eroding, the slopes are covered by a heavy
growth of scrubwood, with deep bracken in the openings.
About half a mile above the village, after passing through

the scar-bound hollow of Lagan Geoidh, the burn plunges into a narrow and formidable chasm, up to a hundred feet deep, the water-course here following a fault in the rock, not making its own valley. Below the foot of the chasm the burn divides to enclose a small island, and then debouches on to a flood-plain only slightly above sea-level and contained to seaward by a storm-beach. It here approaches the lowermost stretch of a smaller and much shorter burn which has run down past the Castle, and about which more will be said on p.83. Until recent years the lowermost reach of the larger burn ran westwards, behind the storm-beach and more or less parallel with the line of the village street, and only turned out into the sea in the corner of the Bay, where a small tributary enters from the Crow Glen; today, however, the situation is entirely changed, as the burn, about 1950, broke out seawards through the storm-beach some two hundred yards further west, making itself a new mouth. Further changes to the course of the burn have been made in recent times.

The Claonaig Burn shows certain analogies with Glen Skibble, though on a larger scale. For example, it also possesses a basin too big for its system of streams following at times faults in the rock, the lowermost portion consisting of a straight and rather deep trough. The basin, which extends in part beyond the bounds of the estate, measures over six miles in greatest width, from Lochan Fraoich to Cruach Tarsuinn, and also forms a kind of wide saddle across the whole peninsula, the lowest point on which is only about 350ft above sea-level. There are several fair-sized tributaries, of which the Larachmor Burn, about three miles long, once supported several crofts. The hills are in general from two to three hundred feet lower than those at the north end of the estate, and much of the valley either is or has at some time been under the plough; the main area of fertile ground is centred on Glenreasdell Mains, at less than three hundred feet above the sea. The trough that forms the lower end of the valley is, as has been said, straight and rather steeply cut, with scrubwood at the base of its flanks.

The rest of the ground, south-west of the Claonaig Burn, calls for no detailed description. It consists of low hills facing the sea, with broken ground behind stretching back to the main watershed. The familiar scrubwood and small farms occupy the lower slopes.

Note: The drawing at the beginning of this chapter shows, top left, Skipness School and, bottom left, fishermen's houses demolished before 1885 for the New Road. It is from a photograph taken between 1868, when the School was built, and 1885.

2. ACCESS BY SEA

Today Skipness is normally approached by land, but this is
due only to the development of modern roads, and until well
on in the nineteenth century most of the traffic was seaborne.
The laird's title-deeds significantly require, or used to require,
the provision of an eight-oared galley for the Duke of Argyll's
use if that worthy should happen to appear. But the business
of getting ashore, except from the smallest craft, must always
have presented a problem. It is true that the Bay is wide, is
free from rocks and boulders, and gives reasonable shelter from
winds with a northerly component; Langlands' map, in fact,
marks an anchorage in its western corner. But it also suffers
from at least two serious drawbacks. The first is its direct
exposure to the prevailing wind, Kilbrannan Sound being
aimed into the very eye of oncoming Atlantic storms. The Bay
then becomes a dangerous lee shore, and even in summer boats
are pulled up well above the reach of the waves when trouble
threatens. My father once had a yacht, but I gather that the
lack of a harbour or sheltered anchorage greatly lessened its
utility. I remember, too, that one summer, perhaps about 1896,
a 'puffer' called the *Polar Light* was caught by a storm when
aground on the beach unloading a cargo of coal, our practice
having been to obtain a year's supply delivered on the shore
and to unload it straight into carts; the vessel remained ashore
for weeks until a tug came and pulled her off, while her crew
camped in the potting-shed at the bottom of the garden. The
second drawback is sand. As the tide goes down a sandy flat
dries out, over which incoming boats have to be dragged before

they reach even the foot of the shingly foreshore. Alternatively, perhaps, they may be left with an anchor ashore and a long rope, to be retrieved when the tide returns, but this can only be risked in really calm weather. My father tried to beat the sand by building a long jetty, but the sea had the last word: the hand-rail went first, and then the wooden footway, while the iron uprights were left standing on their concrete bases ready to punch holes in the bottom of any heedless boat. At last these too sank gradually into the sand and were swallowed up.

Landing-places sheltered from the west, though naturally exposed to the east, can be found from place to place along the coast fronting on Loch Fyne. The first is a small, shallow bay, just north of the rocks that form the base of the Point, which figures as Brann a' Phuirt on the Ordnance maps but is ordinarily called Shell Bay. Improbable as the place may appear as the site of a harbour, signs that it was once so used may be clearly seen. Thus the bay ends on the south in a steep-to rock whose top could have served as a quay, while at its edge there is water alongside, at every high tide, for a boat drawing three to four feet. There are also traces of artificial deepening and clearance, all large stones having been removed and a channel up to two feet deep cut in the rock, and at the edge of the rock three holes have been drilled, to which boats could have been moored. In dangerous easterly weather a boat could have been brought further in, round the corner of the rock, as the artificial channel is prolonged in this direction, and if necessary could have been beached where the channel runs up to dry land. Local tradition has it that a small yacht was berthed there at some time before 1843, but the amount of labour evidently expended on the channel, as well as the degree of wear shown by the holes, makes it probable that the quay was used by small trading craft, which came in on the tide and were worked while lying dry.

Better documented than Shell Bay is Port a' Chruidh, which lies about a mile to the north. The name means the Port of the Cattle, and the final word sounds like 'Chro' to uninstructed ears. With the name should be associated the local tradition of droved cattle being shipped to the mainland, though whether they came from Islay, as one version suggests, or simply from elsewhere in Kintyre does not appear. Islay droves making for Falkirk Tryst were usually ferried over the Point of Knap, in Knapdale, or else to Jura and then, after traversing that island, from its northern end to Craignish; but that some droves should exceptionally have crossed to Kintyre, and have been shipped on from Port a' Chruidh, does not seem impossible. The place was used by ordinary traffic as well: for example, boats crossing to Ayrshire with passengers or goods would make it their point of departure, and Mrs Robert Campbell records having landed there herself in 1813. The actual 'port' is a small shingly inlet in the littoral rocks, with at least one hole for a mooring-rope, like those at Shell Bay, bored through the rock on the south; access from the landward is easy, as the range of Raised Beach rocks is conveniently flattened off. A spring close by has been improved for the benefit of fishermen calling to replenish their water-casks.

In 1838, however, Port a' Chruidh was superseded, and a real harbour, different in kind from the natural rocky inlets, was built about a quarter of a mile further to the north. The object was now to provide a place of refuge for the large number of boats engaged on the herring fishery, and the Fishery Board met one third of the original cost, which amounted to £2977, as well as of an additional £114 8s 3d which was needed later for repairs. The plan and specifications published by the Board show that the work consisted of an angled breakwater-pier running out eastwards from the rocks and then turning north to form a partially enclosed basin measuring some two hundred and fifty by two hundred feet. The masonry was of dressed stone with a hand-packed rubble core, and there was a parapet on the outer edge. A good deal of rock was also cut away along the landward side of the basin. Though sheltered from the west, the site was, of course, totally exposed to the east; the structure was in ruins long before the end of the century, and the last of the well-dressed red stonework was demolished in a gale in 1911.

The New Pier, built by my father in or about the later 1870s, at a cost of £3000, was a deepwater structure intended for the use of steamers. It was built of re-used iron rails, from the Great Western Railway. Its site, nearly two miles north of the village, was chosen in the hope that the daily mailboat would call there on her run between the Kyles of Bute and Tarbert; this never happened, but the pier was served by a small cargo-vessel, the *Minard Castle*, which ran on alternate days between Glasgow and Inveraray. The service, however, was precarious, as no call could be made in an easterly wind of more than moderate strength, particularly if the tide was either very low or very high, as in the former case the ship could have bumped on the bottom in a trough between two waves and in the latter could have been deposited squarely on top of the pier. Nor was there anything remotely resembling a timetable. A traveller, due to embark for South America the following day from the Clyde, was once left stranded on the pier when the *Minard* was unable to call, and had to be rowed over to Bute in a small boat to catch the mail-steamer at Rothesay. Captain McGugan was a firm friend of our family; he treated his passengers as guests and probably felt that to make a charge for a ticket was a breach of Highland manners. At the end of his service he retired to Inveraray, where he died in fairly recent years at the age of ninety-four.

The new pier had to be served by a proper road, replacing the old track to Culindrach, and my father accordingly built one onwards from the end of the highway. This may at the time have been some two hundred yards north of Monybackach, where the O.S. map of 1867 marks the highway as giving place to the Culindrach track. The further distance from this point was about a mile and a half, and a dated photograph shows that the southern part at least was complete by 1877. The straight stretch across the marshy ground south-east of Laggan is said to have been founded on logs, as ordinary bottoming tended to sink into the moss; the old track had overcome this difficulty by making a detour to the west, and keeping to the lowermost part of the drier rising ground.

With the coming of motor transport the pier's utility waned, its maintenance, at the same time, began to grow more and more costly, and it was finally given up in the 1930s. In my boyhood tremendous dramas were enacted at the pier when sheep had to be embarked, on the *Minard* or a chartered vessel, for their period of wintering in the Lowlands. If one or two could be dragged on board along the gangway, and a few more chivvied after them to set an example, there was hope that the rest might follow in an orderly manner, but enormous efforts were needed on the part of shepherds, ship's crew, bystanders, children and dogs, and the danger always remained of a sheep or two breaking back, escaping along the road, or even falling into the sea. A much more peaceful memory is that of fishing, on calm days, for the very small fish that lived underneath the pier, flicking in and out of the seaweed that grew on the iron uprights.

The northernmost 'port' on the estate was Altagalvash Bay, a mile north of the pier. It is surely an index of the toughness of the early nineteenth century that this could have seemed a suitable place for landing, as it entailed a longish and very rough walk through wild country; but passengers from Tarbert evidently did sometimes land there, and in 1814 Mrs Robert Campbell alludes to 'the Tarbert pacquet', suggesting a regular service between Loch Fyne and the Kyles of Bute. Crossings to Bute, from one point or another on the Skipness side, seem on her evidence to have been common enough, as, for example, on an occasion in January 1814, when 'a priest' – Mrs Campbell was a Catholic – 'left this evening for Bute in a small open boat containing, besides himself, twelve people and eight casks of whisky'.

The small inlets along the coast south-west of the village, and the larger bay into which the Claonaig Burn debouches, were probably of little consequence except to fishermen and to the so-called 'gravel stealers', who sailed about in big smacks and dug themselves cargoes of gravel from other people's beaches. An exception, however, may have been the very small bay of Brian Phort, near Eascairt, which is likely to have served as a water-gate to the stack-built dun described on p.27.

No castaway is known or reported to have reached the shore by swimming, but a stag once nearly did so. One night some fishermen observed an object swimming in the middle of the Sound, and noticing that it had horns were afraid that it might be the devil; however, they netted it and found that it was only a stag, apparently crossing over to Kintyre from Arran. It was turned loose, on the hill, and presumably continued its journey.

3. ACCESS BY LAND

The first road in Kintyre for which any records exist is the portage between East and West Tarbert. This has been the scene of two Royal escapades. Magnus Barefoot of Norway, having been granted the Hebrides in 1098, wished to add Kintyre to them by proving it to be an island, and to this end he had his ship hauled across from one sea to the other. Robert Bruce repeated the performance in the 1320s, to demonstrate his power to the Lord of the Isles and other interested parties; but he made the mistake of having the sail hoisted, with the result that the ship was blown off the road and crashed. The place, which is still known as Lag na Luing (the Hollow of the Ship), is close to the Tarbert church hall. The existence of the portage, however, tells us nothing about routes serving the rest of the peninsula, and for that matter as late as 1734 Cowley's map of the Duke of Argyll's dukedom marked no roads anywhere south of Inveraray. Roy's map of Scotland (1747-55) marks the road from the north not as running direct from Lochgilphead to Tarbert but as making a detour by Loch Caolisport, crossing from Ormsary to West Loch Tarbert and turning the head of the latter with a branch to East Tarbert. From the head of the loch a road is shown running, as today, along the west coast of Kintyre, with the branch-road to Skipness striking off it at Lagvoulin Inn, now Redhouse. Cowley's omission of these roads may safely be attributed to oversight or error, as they are unlikely to have come into existence in the twenty years that separated his work from that of Roy.

The word 'road' as used in the last few sentences should be

14

taken with a grain of salt, as those shown by Roy, or some of them, may well have been no better than customary tracks, lacking any kind of improvement. This is not, of course, to overlook the fact that, in many places, roads were being actively improved, and turnpikes organised, at the time of Roy's survey; in the case of Kintyre, however, grounds for suspicion are provided by Roy himself. Thus while his road from Redhouse up to and over the watershed, and thence down towards Glenreasdell Mains, corresponds colourably with the highway of later times, at Glenreasdell Mains he marks it, without any change in character, as splitting into two branches, neither of which can ever have been more than a crude hill-track. One is therefore bound to suspect that the whole of the branch from Redhouse may have been in the same condition, even if the coastwise road from Tarbert to Campbeltown had been more or less improved – as to which point, however, nothing is known. Twenty-five years later things may have changed for the better, as Taylor and Skinner's Road-book, published in 1776, shows the Campbeltown road as a regular highway, and the end of the Skipness branch-road that joins it at Redhouse is clearly marked; and it is possible that the building of a church at Claonaig in 1756 may have encouraged the heritors to provide proper access. When allowance is made for the difference in scale, Roy's line from Redhouse as far as Glenreasdell Mains agrees very fairly with the one shown on the Ordnance maps, and in fact the fairly straight course of B8001 is natural enough, as it encounters one obstacle serious enough to affect it; this is the Gartavaigh Burn, where the difficulty has been met in the eighteenth-century manner with a hairpin bend and a sharp turn on to a bridge. Considering that this road at its highest point is hardly more than four hundred feet above the sea, the views that it gives both to west and to east are most notable – to the west the Paps of Jura, in an aspect only less striking than the one that they present to Cboc a' Bhaile Shios, and to the east an Arran differing remarkably from the one that is seen from Skipness. To a Skipness eye, in fact, it seems definitely wrong, as the Cock of Arran has displaced Millstone Point at the left-hand end of the mass, and has thereby spoiled the balance and dignity of the whole composition.

At Glenreasdell Mains, as has been said, Roy marks the road as forking: a left branch bearing slightly south of east towards Skipness and a right branch crossing the Claonaig Burn, which Roy calls the 'Water of Glen Risdale', and running along the hillside parallel to its right bank. He marks no road along the left side of Claonaig Glen, to correspond with the present further course of the B8001. The right-hand branch has no bearing on the subject of access to Skipness, as on reaching the mouth of the glen it turns away south-westwards, along the coast, as the prototype of B842; but an unmade road on its line can be traced through the scrubwoods on the west side of the glen, ending at Creggan farm. Roy's east-going branch, however, possesses a good deal of interest, as it approximates to a well-established hill-track from Glenreasdell Mains to Skipness. The distance is less than three miles, the going is easy, by a neck about three hundred feet above sea-level, and a stretch of the uppermost part has actually been improved for traffic by a bottoming of large stones; while the cairn on the summit, if it is not simply a prehistoric monument like the cist on the neighbouring hillside, may well be a direction-cairn such as is often seen beside Border drove-roads. In addition, the track has found a place in local folklore, as an old woman once told my father that St Columba preached to the people of Skipness from the summit, adding that the saint, while he lived in Ireland, had been a Roman Catholic, but that on coming to Scotland had become a Presbyterian. Today the track reaches Skipness by way of Caolfin, but before the enclosures and planting of the nineteenth century its course could have been more direct; Roy's map suggests that it reached the Skipness Burn below the foot of the chasm, crossed it perhaps at the island, though no traces of a ford exist there or anywhere, and continued thence to the Castle; he marks no houses on the present site of the village, so a direct course to the Castle would seem logical enough.

A further point to be recalled in relation to this track is that it connects with and prolongs an easy route from the west coast of Kintyre. This route crosses over from Clachan in a more or less straight line, and is mentioned or implied more than once in Mrs Higginson's notes. The fact that the parish church was at Clachan until 1753, when Skipness was disjoined from Kilcalmonell and Kilberry, may have helped to increase the traffic; and in earlier days, before Argyll was Campbellised, communications with Islay and the south may have had particular importance.

The situation recorded by Roy probably changed soon after his survey was made. When Skipness was disjoined from Kilcalmonell and Kilberry, Saddell was similarly disjoined from Killean and a new parish of Saddell and Skipness was formed. A church to serve it was built at Claonaig in 1756, 'Cluneg' (Roy) or 'Clunaig' (Langlands) having been in Roy's day a small group of houses, probably a multiple farm, a short distance south-east of the church site. It was probably these changes that led to the next step in the development of the local roads. Whether or no this was part of a single large operation, covering the whole of the route from Redhouse onwards, Langlands' map of Argyllshire, of 1801, shows a system almost the same as the one that exists today. That is to say, the prototype of B8001 has been pushed forward from Glenreasdell Mains along the eastern side of the glen, the Claonaig Burn has been bridged south of the church, and the east-coast road to Saddell and Campbeltown has been aligned on the new bridge. At the same time, the old 'High Road', now largely abandoned, has been built from the church to Skipness, with its final stretch apparently following what is now the village street though no village is indicated. (The history of the village will be discussed in Chapter 8.)

Comments on the roads in this stage of their development are provided by two contributors to the *Statistical Account of Scotland*, both writing in 1794. The minister of Saddell and Skipness says in part 'The roads here are very good, and are kept in good repair: they were made partly by statute-work, and partly by the voluntary contributions of the gentlemen', though a stent (or levy) was also required; and he adds that three large and three small bridges had been made on the east-coast route but that four large ones and four small ones were still needed. He states further that the east-coast route was part of the 'great line' from Inveraray to Campbeltown, though admitting that 'another line' existed on the west side; but this should perhaps be regarded as a piece of local patriotism, seeing that the west-coast route was already organised in the days of Taylor and Skinner. The minister of Kilcalmonell and Kilberry likewise gives a good mark to the Redhouse-Claonaig road, the western end of which lay in his parish. By modern standards, however, there is much to seek in the quality of the east-coast road, as it is narrow, twisty and switch-back; when roadside AA signs were first put up, about 1912, it was allotted one only, at Claonaig, to serve the whole of its length, and this read 'Dangerous Throughout'.

The approach to Skipness from the west and south assumed its final form in the 1870s or '80s, when my father built a 'New Road', at sea-level, to supersede the old 'High Road' from Claonaig to the western end of the village. This was done partly to provide relief work at a time of agricultural depression.

This low-level road was a favourite resort for tinkers, just as in 1848, when cholera was epidemic in Glasgow, numbers of refugees found their way to the caves and rock-shelters along this stretch of the coast. The tinkers came and went in family groups, generally travelling with a pony and cart and camping by the roadside in longish, low tents with a framework of arched rods. They also made use of a cave, really a rock-shelter formed by a great slab of rock slipped from the face of a bluff, at a point about half a mile short of the end of the village; the entrance to the shelter had been narrowed with drystone walling, and a small burn ran close by. Two clans of tinkers were mainly represented, Townsleys and Williamsons, and the commonness of red hair suggested Irish blood; they certainly showed no Gypsy traits, and some groups contained a piper. Some of them collected winkles, which they shipped in sacks to Billingsgate. One old man, perhaps not a member of a gang, was credited with being a veteran of the Crimean War. It was said that new-born tinker babies were dipped in a running burn, on the principle of 'kill or cure'; and the doctor was once heard to say that the excellence of the women's hair was due to the fact that they habitually washed it in sheep-dip, presumably stolen from fanks. A great sensation was caused during the First World War by the award of a decoration to a tinker whose mother, a Mrs MacColl, was in residence in the rock-shelter when the news came out; my sister Mrs Gordon called on her formally there to offer congratulations. In a different class was Mrs Bunce, as she conducted a legitimate business in handmade wickerwork chairs. She lived somewhere in the English Midlands, cut the withies and made the chairs in winter, and spent the summer touring with a van and selling them from door to door.

So much for the approaches from the west, but nothing has yet been said about direct access from the north, and, with Tarbert only eight miles away as the crow flies, strangers sometimes questioned the detour by Redhouse and Claonaig. Some strangers did more than question, as hopeful summer visitors have been known to start out from Tarbert to walk along the shore to Skipness, only to arrive battered, exhausted and drenched in the small hours of the following morning. The shoreline is not, in fact, a practicable route, much of it being bedevilled by steep rocks and seamed with clefts and gullies which leave no space for a pathway above the tide-mark; while the walker who climbs up inland in the hope of easier going finds himself confronted at one point by a transverse wall of cliff which can only be turned at some four hundred feet above the sea. Anyone therefore who elects to follow this route must accept a substantial climb, start out of Tarbert by a track which rises behind the town, attain a height where the burns are still too small to have cut out their beds into gullies, and skirt the upper edge of the scrubwoods. At the Skipness march-burn, a branch of Allt Gamhna, he will pass an enormous boulder set

upright on a very steep slope and measuring thirteen feet in
height on its downhill side; its purpose may simply have been
to identify the march-burn, but it could equally have served
as a direction marker to indicate the lowest elevation at which
it was advisable to travel, and if this route was ever used for
droving cattle, such a marker might well have been needed.
The Lord High Treasurer's Accounts record that in 1326
cattle were driven to Skipness on two occasions ('in fugacione
martorum . . . per duas vices'), at a total cost of eightpence,
but nothing is said as to the route that the drover followed;
however, as the Redhouse route is unlikely to have been in
any way improved at such an early date, even if it existed at
all, he may well have come direct. The transport of bread to
Skipness, for which twenty-two pence were paid in the same
year, may or may not have been by sea.

The track leading out of Tarbert that has just been
mentioned is said locally to have been made by some former
laird of Stonefield as part of a projected direct road to Skipness,
but to have been abandoned when the laird of Skipness was
unwilling to share in the work. His unwillingness was natural
enough, in view of the nature of the terrain; my father looked
into a similar project in the later nineteenth century, at a time
when all prices were low, and was given an estimate of £1000
per mile.

The best route, in fact, is not along the sea-face at all, but
over the watershed – best, that is to say, for the unimpeded
walker, though impossible for droved cattle on account of
the mosses and bog-holes. The going is better, the extra
elevation is moderate, and the actual distance is shorter,
being the chord instead of the arc. The walker may swim
in the lochs, may satisfy himself that the islet in the smaller
loch is not a crannog, and may possibly come across a pair of
red-throated divers nesting. On the larger loch he may find
the remains of the sluice that was used to send extra water
down the burn to work the mill at Skipness. The practice may
have been less inefficient than it sounds, as a very old plumber
once told me how the town of Dunbar was saved from drought

in a rather similar way. In his youth the town had no proper
water-supply, but shared with a farmer a reservoir far up in the
Lammermuirs, and one very dry summer the farmer refused
to give Dunbar its share. However, the town's plumber, my
informant's master, sent him up to the reservoir night after
night to remove a certain brick from the dam, and water off for
a stated time into the channel that served the town; he did this
successfully for weeks, and the farmer never caught him.

Further down the burn one sometimes saw a ring-ouzel, and
ravens sometimes nested in the Ravens' Glen in spite of keepers
and shepherd. Below the ravens' nesting-place, again, where
the valley has begun to drop away and the scene has become
less stark, the remains of beehive huts, as described below
on pp.28–9, begin to appear in groups and lines along the
burnside; notwithstanding their archaic appearance, they were
probably shielings, and need not be older than the eighteenth
or early nineteenth century. It is probably these huts that have
given an adjoining glen its Ordnance Survey name of Gleann
Baile na h-Uamha (*uamh*, cave or den). Following the burn
downstream from the huts, the walker will reach the forks, and
on the opposite side from the abandoned Glenskibble house
he will find one of the Bronze-Age monuments mentioned in
Chapter 5, a large cup-marked boulder. Below the forks, on
his last lap to Skipness, he will benefit from the track that
once led to the abandoned house, and will appreciate the
mettle of the children of successive shepherds, who dutifully
walked their two miles to school along it daily, and two miles
back, in all seasons and weathers. Beside the track, near the
point where it begins to rise from the bank of the burn, there
used to lie a flattish slab of rock with a round hole in its
surface, apparently an unfinished millstone abandoned in the
course of manufacture. Another unsuccessful attempt to make
a millstone may be seen in a cutting in a rock-face about 350
yards south of the top of Cnoc an t-Suidhe (883581).

In winter, it need hardly be said, the watershed route might
bear a different complexion. Mrs. Higginson records that a
postwoman, one Christina MacSim, was lost in the snow

somewhere near the Stonefield march on her way from Tarbert with the mails, and was buried where she was found; and I myself remember a boy having died of exposure when lost with his father in a blizzard somewhere in the region. Another version of the story of the postwoman, locally current, placed her death on the track leading from Glenreasdell, and identified the cairn on the summit (p.24) as her grave, but Mrs. Higginson's account is the more probable.

4. ACCESS BY AIR

The only report of a landing at Skipness from the air relates to Eagle's Bay, a small inlet in the littoral rocks between the village and Claonaig Bay. It is folklore, and deserves to be set out in Mrs Higginson's own words. 'Below Goirteaneorna', she writes,

> is a small port in the shore rocks called Eagle Port in Gaelic Poirte na h-Iolaire. Many years ago on harvest day when the shearers were busy shearing their corn in Goirteaneorna they noticed a very bulky thing flying over the sea from the direction of Caticol in Arran. They were watching it flying across and they seen it was an enormous bird. They went down to the shore to have a better view of it. In its claws it was carrying something bulky, it let itself rest on the rocks in this little port and it dropped its burden on the rock it was a small infant. The people at once secured the child and took it home with them, it was a wee girl. Not long after the eagle left it a boat was seen crossing over from Arran after it. They found their child all right at Goirteaneorna. It happened that the Arran people were harvesting in the field, the mother wrapping the baby in a shawl and leaving it sleeping behind a stook of corn when the eagle snatched it away.

The Gaelic form of the place-name, as quoted by Mrs Higginson, shows that it really does derive from an eagle, real or legendary, and not, like Gleneagles in Perthshire, from a church (*eaglais*). For that matter, no church exists, or has ever existed as far as anyone can tell, anywhere near Eagle's Bay.

5. THE OLDEST INHABITANTS

To form any picture of the people who have formed the community of Skipness in the past, it is necessary to begin at a very distant date. The Castle, as will be explained in a later chapter, originated only in the early thirteenth century, but remains of one sort or another survive in the neighbourhood which show that men have lived here for four millennia or longer. This is not surprising in view of the natural advantages that the place offered to really primitive people, who would have found deer to supply meat, skins for clothing and tents, bone and antler for tools, and sinew for cordage and thread; hares and winged game if they could snare it; salmon and sea-trout, to be netted at the mouths of the burns in summer and autumn; sea-fish at most other seasons when a canoe could venture out; shellfish and the long-shore oddments that the Orcadians neatly call 'ebb-meat'; and woods for fuel and shelter. For farmers, at a later stage, there was cultivable soil, particularly where they had cut and burned the woods, with grazing on the lower hill-slopes; while the game and fish, as before, no doubt eked out deficiencies in all the prehistoric periods.

The following early monuments are known at Skipness. (For a full description, see the Ancient Monuments Commission's *Inventory of the Ancient Monuments of Argyll, I, Kintyre*.)

Chambered cairn. Multiple burial in more or less elongated cairns or mounds was a rite typical of the neolithic people who introduced agriculture into Britain in the third millennium BC, and one of their cairns can be seen south-east of Glenreasdell Mains (864582). This example is placed by

24

experts in a group peculiar to the Firths of Clyde and Solway. Today it takes the form of a nearly circular mound of large stones and earth, about fifty feet in diameter, with remains of two, or perhaps three, slab-built burial-chambers appearing on the surface and traces of upright blocks here and there on the circumference. It has, however, been very severely robbed, as it is dangerously close to farm buildings and a main road – in fact, sixty years ago the best-preserved chamber, which is eight feet long by two feet eight inches wide, harboured the shepherd's pig – but originally it was presumably longish or wedge-shaped, the chambers being set in the thicker end, and it is only the wasted remains of this thicker end that now survive.

Other cairns and cists. It is probably pointless to draw too hard a line between cairns which seem intact and may or may not contain, or cover, a cist, ruined cairns with remains of a cist inside them, and cists now lying bare, from over which a cairn or mound may or may not have been removed. The experts are in any case chary of dating either cists or cairns when no relics have been found inside them, and are apt to speak guardedly of the second millennium BC. The Ancient Monuments Commissioners accept two cairns, Cnoc na Sgratha (885579) and Eas Faolain (906588); a third, which is marked as an antiquity on the Ordnance maps, is most probably a guide-cairn beside an old road (p.16). There are also six cists, a single one near the top of the Crow Glen (892583) and a scattered group of five near Glenreasdell Mains (centrally 859582). The cairns are respectively twenty-five and fifteen feet in diameter and the cists are generally something under four feet long. The remains of one of the Glenreasdell group belong to the rather restricted class in which the side-slabs are grooved, to allow the end-slabs to be fitted in neatly.

Cup-marked stones. Kintyre is notably rich in stones and rock-faces bearing assemblages of small round hollows, sometimes encircled by rings. Thirteen are known near Skipness, of which the best is on the opposite side of the burn from the abandoned Glenskibble house, and a short distance south-east of the forks (892600); fifty years ago at least forty-one could be counted, with less definite traces of some fifteen more. Another good example, a slab of rock showing traces of at least twenty-five cups, lies about sixty yards north-east of Eas Faolain, the burn that runs down from the reservoir, at a point three hundred and twenty yards above the Pier Road (906587). The rest are recorded as follows by the Ancient Monuments Commissioners: Altagalvash (902615, 912617), Claonaig (869570), Culindrach (917516), Gleann Baile na h-Uamha (895614), Glenbuie (889577), Glenreasdell Mains (851589, 864580), Home Farm (914581), Larachmor Burn (843575), the Manse (896575), Oragaig (850545). The experts are far from definite about the origin and purpose of these markings, but a Bronze Age date is agreed, in the second millennium BC. One engaging theory connects them with putative incomers from south-western Europe, prospecting for copper of gold.

Duns. There are two small duns in the area, Dunan Breac overlooking the chasm in the lower part of Glen Skibble and another, nameless and only recently discovered by the Ancient Monuments Commission, on the shore near Eascairt farm. An Dunan, by the western end of the village, though marked on the Ordnance map in Gothic characters, is a purely natural feature.

Dunan Breac (898582) stands on the top of a mound which backs on a high precipice, and is enclosed on its other sides by a crescent-shaped hollow. By the standards of its time this position was reasonably strong, in spite of higher ground close by beyond the hollow, as the mound sloped steeply enough to check the end of a rush while the danger of plunging fire, of arrows or sling-stones, does not seem to have greatly troubled the builders of any duns. Being, like most duns, without an internal wall, it was naturally in no position to stand a siege, but again this drawback is likely to have been discounted, as the military science of enemies and bad neighbours would probably not have run to more than a heroic assault. The wall, of rather rough dry masonry, is now wasted to ground-level; fragments of its outer face can be found among the debris that covers the flanks of the mound, but no part of the inner face has been preserved and a wall-thickness of about ten feet can therefore only be guessed at. No walling appears along the lip of the precipice where this is enclosed in the work; if any ever existed it has no doubt been carried away by the erosion of the cliff-face below. The interior measures about fifty-eight feet in diameter, and some trial pits dug in it showed remains of rough paving, probably at two levels, with much discolouration by charcoal. The position of the entrance is uncertain. The only significant relics recovered in a partial excavation were two quartzite pebbles each marked with a linear groove; 'strike-lights' of this type occur pretty commonly in brochs, and in other buildings of the early years of our era.

The other dun is on top of an isolated stack of rock, five hundred yards east-north-east of Eascairt (848536), and only thirty-five yards from high-water mark. The stack overlooks a small inlet marked Brian Phort on the maps, is twenty-five feet high, and provides on its summit a habitable space which measures only fifty-five by thirty-five feet. The whole of this space was occupied by the dun, the plan of which it dictated as the wall simply followed its lip all round. The thickness of the wall is uncertain, but may have been about seven or eight feet. Stacks of this kind are not unusual sites for small strongholds, and may well have given useful protection against casual thieves or raiders; this one evidently possessed the additional advantage of being close to a shingly beach, off which a boat could have been worked.

This chapter began as an account of the pre-mediaeval remains, but it will be convenient for practical purposes to waive this proviso and to include some monuments whose origins are just as obscure as those of the cairns and duns though most, if not all, of them are likely to be of fairly recent date.

Hut-circles. This district is full of the remains of very small buildings of turf, or turf and stone, sometimes standing singly but more often in groups, and always extremely dilapidated.

They are of various shapes and sizes – round, square, oblong, oblong with rounded corners, irregular – and may be single or subdivided into two or three rooms; others again consist of two contiguous circles not communicating with one another. The doorways are always very narrow and are often flanked by slabs set on edge; sometimes they are placed in a corner if the plan is rectangular. The huts are chiefly notable for their very small size; the largest measure internally only about eighteen feet by six feet, while some of the smallest circles are as little as four feet in diameter. Their appearance is thus very primitive, but local tradition connects them with the system of summer grazing, which persisted here well into the first half of the nineteenth century. Under it, the cattle were taken to the hill-pastures in the early summer by the women, who lived in the shielings and made the milk into cheese. The huts tend to occur on lower-lying or partially sheltered sites, often along burns; they are so numerous that a complete list would outrun the scope of this work, but a few examples will illustrate their general character.

(a)   A group of thirty-three huts, known to have been used as a shieling until fairly recent times, stands on a bluff on the east side of Glen Skibble about eight hundred and fifty yards below the forks (892594). The rings of turf walling, two or three feet thick, stand about a foot high, and are generally founded on a low mound. Most are round or oblong, with internal dimensions varying from four feet to twelve feet; the entrances are from two feet to three feet wide, and many are flanked with upright slabs.

(b)   More than a mile further from civilisation, in Glean Baile na h-Uamha (895615), there is a settlement of nineteen huts divided into three groups, one on a knoll, another on the opposite side of the burn, and the third a hundred yards away, higher up the hillside. The huts show most of the types of plan described, and none is larger than twelve feet by six feet. One of the cup-marked stones described above lies on the side of the knoll, perhaps put there for luck; and a pathway has been marked out with upright stones to a crossing-place on the burn.

(c) A group, which would really have amounted to a considerable village if all the huts had been occupied at the same time, lies on and near a burn-junction (Allt Ruadh and Allt Leum nam Meann) a mile and a half north-west of Gartavaigh (c.870603). The huts show most of the ordinary features of their class, with the following individual points – most appear to be wholly or largely of stone, the oblong plan is commoner than the round, very small circles are absent, double huts are rare and only one has three rooms. Two of the huts have been excavated. One gave little information except that it had been inhabited at two main periods, the floor being remade between them, and that in the second occupation, at least, a good deal of iron had been smelted. The other showed several layers of disconnected occupation, but the discovery of a fragment of green-glazed pottery cannot be regarded as proof of a mediaeval date.

Enclosure. No obvious explanation suggests itself for the remains of an enclosure on a bluff overlooking the former site of the farm of Laggan (906590), but in some late phase of its history it seems to have been associated with a corn-drying kiln. It measures about fifty feet by thirty feet, and the entrance, which is six feet wide at narrowest, is flanked by stone slabs on edge.

Miscellaneous stones. Although there are no pillar-like 'standing stones' at Skipness, stone slabs and blocks not bearing cup-marks occur which have clearly been set up artificially in their present positions. The most striking of these has already been mentioned on p.20, where it was cited as a boundary stone or a direction marker. Nothing would be gained by listing all those which have come to notice, but readily accessible examples may be seen

(a) about fifty yards east of the lowermost corner of the Chapel Wood (912575) or

(b) near the second of the cup-marked slabs mentioned above.

At this latter site there are two erect stones and two fallen ones, arranged in line in such a way as to suggest that they may be the grounders of a vanished turf-dyke.

Bloomeries. Bloomeries consist of mounds or deposits of slag, cinders and charcoal resulting from the reduction of iron-ore by a primitive process. This entailed no more than the heating of the ore in a charcoal fire, well surrounded by or bedded into the fuel, and the metal that was obtained could easily be forged at red heat into a bar of iron. The heyday of iron-smelting in the West Highlands seems to have begun in the second quarter of the eighteenth century, when English ironmasters took to shipping their ore to districts where fuel was available in the form of standing woods, and smelting it there, the first furnace of this class having been opened at Invergarry in 1727. It may be remarked here in passing that the Invergarry operations resulted in something of much greater ultimate importance than a certain tonnage of iron, in that the company's resident manager, one Thomas Rawlinson from Lancashire, invented the kilt as we know it; finding the traditional belted plaid (*feileadhmor*) inconvenient for work in the woods, he cut it in half, discarded the upper part, and pleated the lower part round the waist and thighs in the manner of a modern kilt (*feileadh-beag*). The bloomeries at Skipness – unlike, for example, those on the north-east bank of Loch Lomond – are too few and scattered to suggest an organised industry, and point rather to the activities of ordinary smiths working the deposits of bog-iron that were available locally. On this showing they are likely to be earlier rather than later than the eighteenth-century period of industrial exploitation.

At least seven bloomeries have been positively identified at or near Skipness and several others have been reported. They are in various states of preservation, the best consisting of a mound of slag associated with a hut and a platform for the making of charcoal (*infra*). This example is on the left bank of a small unmarked burn in the wood named on the maps

Coille Rudha Dhuibh (861551), and fifty years ago could be found without much difficulty as its site was in the middle of a ride a short distance above the cliffs. Other examples are either poorly preserved or are difficult of access.

Charcoal-burning. Charcoal was prepared on platforms, sometimes called 'pitsteads', dug out from the hillside and levelled, and assemblages of these platforms occur in three different areas, all covered with scrubwood. These areas are respectively on the sea-face overlooking Loch Fyne north of the former site of Skipness Pier, in Claonaig Glen, and on the slopes below the highway between Claonaig and Eascairt. The platforms are generally oval, and about twenty feet long; charred wood is generally to be found under the turf that covers them. No doubt the charcoal-burners cut the scrubwoods and made the charcoal on the spot, shipping it to the foundries by sea; it was observed that the coastal sites were at heights of less than two hundred and fifty feet, which would have facilitated direct loading wherever boats could put in. A probable outlet for charcoal from Skipness would have been the Goatfield ironworks at Furnace, near Inveraray; these were in operation from 1775 to 1813, and the latter date would agree well enough with the probable age of some coppiced oaks at Claonaig.

6. THE CASTLE

It is sobering to realise that, from the end of Dunan Breac to
the beginning of the Castle, there is a gap of perhaps as much as
a thousand years, and that nothing can be cited with confidence
to fill it up. It is true that some of the huts, presented above
as shielings of pretty recent date, may really be Dark Age
dwellings, but this is the merest surmise. It is also true that the
men who, in 1880, were digging trenches for the foundations
of the New House, came on what they said was a ditch filled
up with soil; but my father was away from home, the matter
was never pursued, and consequently, however attractive may
be the idea of a Dark Age earthwork, or even a motte, on the
site, nothing can be made of this story. The gap must therefore
be accepted, and the Skipness record resumed only in the early
years of the thirteenth century, to which date the experts assign
the oldest construction in the Castle.

To the casual visitor the Castle may appear as a great
rectangular fortress, with a citadel-tower in the north-east
corner for a last desperate defence; but close examination
will show him that this impression is far from the truth. The
Castle as it stands is in fact a complex structure, formed by
a long process of accretion and alteration, and it can only be
understood if the several phases of the process are described
in order. The task of analysis is made harder by the fact that
all the internal buildings were destroyed in the eighteenth
century, when the interior was converted to farm-buildings.
The steading, in its turn, was cleared out by my father in
1898, and the surviving old work left visible.

The oldest buildings on the site were a hall-house* and a chapel, both of which were enclosed within the curtain-wall when this came to be built. All parts of the structure rest on very slight foundations, nowhere more than 30cm in depth. The hall-house occupied the north-west corner of the present enclosure, and three of its walls still stand – its west gable and north side being adapted as parts of the curtain and its east gable serving as the west wall of the building, now topped by the tower, in the north-east corner of the enclosure. The south wall has been pulled down, but a fragment of it survives on the east, returning from the corner now embodied in the north-eastern building, and a scar can be seen where its other end joined the curtain on the west. Like the rest of the Castle it is built of local mica-schist rubble, with red-sandstone dressings identified as coming from Arran; probable sources for the rubble may be seen in a rockface in the Chapel Wood about a quarter of a mile away to the east, or in a raised-beach gully just east of the wood which seems to have been greatly enlarged, as if by use as a quarry. The house measures fifty-six by thirty-six feet overall, and a plinth runs all round the outside. Originally it contained three storeys, though nothing survives of the top one except part of the east gable, incorporated in the building to the east; the ground-floor was probably cellarage, and the whole of the first-floor was probably devoted to the hall, with access by an outside stair on the face of the vanished south wall. The window-openings have round arches inside, and down-sloping heads. The dais was probably at the west end of the hall, in view of the presence there of a two-light window, and of a mural garderobe in the north-west corner. The walls, being between six and seven feet in thickness, could have carried a parapet-walk. A well, just inside the east gable, probably served the hall-house, though the wooden pump-tree

* Facts additional to, or correcting errors in, a paper by the late Professor R.G. Collingwood and myself in *P.S.A.S.* lvii (1922-3), 266ff. have been taken from the account in R.C.A.H.M.S. Argyll 1 Kintyre pp.165-68.

found when it was opened in 1898 was no doubt of much later date.

The builder of the house is unknown, but he was doubtless one of Somerled's family or adherents. In 1261, Dufgal, son of Syfyn, who was at that time lord of Kintyre, alluding in a charter to his 'castle of Schepehinche', no doubt referred to this building. In the early thirteenth century Skipness must have been dangerously placed between the King of Scots and the Lord of the Isles, and a stone-built hall, preferably roofed with some material other than thatch, would have been a valuable possession, particularly on a site so open to the uninvited. The Castle, in fact, stands only some two hundred and thirty yards from high-water mark in Skipness Bay, the slope from the sea being easy and quite free of natural obstacles; and one can thus readily imagine a thatched hall of wood-and-wattle construction disastrously alight within minutes of bad neighbours stealing ashore in the dark. The late Dr W. Douglas Simpson suggested that Alexander II, having defeated Somerled's grandsons in 1222 and established the Crown's position, at least for the time, may have installed men of his own to hold the conquered lands; and a new lord established in a former enemy's territory would certainly have needed a strong house. However that may be, the Ancient Monuments Commissioners state that the hall-house is one of the earliest of its class in Scotland, though contemporary or earlier examples are known among the fortified manor-houses of England. Dr Simpson cited, among possible Scottish parallels, the castles of Raith, Hailes, Tulliallan and Morton.

The chapel stood some fifty yards to the south. It was no doubt intimately associated with the lord's hall, but the place may have had some earlier ecclesiastical connection as excavations, carried out in 1966 by the Ancient Monuments Commissioners, revealed some Christian burials in the south-west corner of the Castle enclosure. All that remains of the chapel today is its south wall incorporated in the Castle's south curtain. It appears to have been about sixty-two feet long by twenty-six feet wide, including a wall-thickness of about three feet nine inches. The chancel was lighted by three windows with heads like those in the hall-house; east of the windows can be seen the remains of a piscina, and just west of the western jamb of the Castle's main entrance, which breaks through the chapel wall, traces of the western jamb of the chapel's own south door. I remember very clearly my father's delight when the demolition of what had been the barn in the old farm-buildings revealed the piscina, which in turn identified that part of the Castle as a chapel; and how it was explained to me that the three niches in the wall were really windows, blocked up by the thickening of the wall on the outer side when the curtain was built and greater thickness was needed for the higher wall. The chapel was dedicated to St Columba, and by his charter of 1261 (*supra*) Dufgal granted it to Paisley Abbey, describing it as 'situated close to my castle of Schepehinche' (*capella Sancti Columbe que sita est juxta castrum meum de Schepehinche*); this grant was endorsed in the following year by the Earl of Menteith, who had in the meanwhile acquired the lands of Skipness from Dufgal. When the incorporation of the chapel in the new castle of enceinte destroyed it as a place of worship, compensation would have had to be made to the Paisley monks, and this is no doubt what led to the building of the new chapel, described in the next chapter.

Nothing is known about the circumstances under which the new large castle was built, but the date is set by the Ancient Monuments Commissioners at the end of the thirteenth or beginning of the fourteenth century. Dr Simpson saw its origin in the war in which Edward I sided with the Lord of the Isles against aggression by the MacDougalls of Lorn, suggested that English masons had been employed, and believed that the place was occupied by a Plantagenet force; he also pointed to the convenient position of Skipness for communication by sea with such places as Dumbarton, Rothesay or Ayr, all held by English garrisons. This advantage the site certainly possessed, as well as excellent observation right down the Sound of Kilbrannan, though it lacked the outstanding strategic advantage of Tarbert, with a sheltered anchorage on both seas and the short portage between them. The paucity of the references to Skipness in the Treasurer's Accounts of 1326 (p.20) shows that Bruce took little interest in the place during his work on Tarbert Castle.

The enlargement of the castle, in the opinion of the Ancient Monuments Commissioners, must have been planned as a whole, but is likely to have taken several years to complete. They believe that in the first stage of the programme the west and north curtains were completed, with their towers, and the east curtain continued south as far as the north-east corner of the chapel. Subsequently the south curtain was carried east as far as the south-east corner of the chapel, the original south wall of the latter being largely retained and heightened. The gatehouse would have been constructed as part of the same operation. Lastly the east gable of the chapel was removed and the south-east tower erected. The courtyard buildings were probably completed at about the same time, the north wall of the chapel being perhaps retained to form the inner wall of the south range. The existence of the hall-house and chapel has affected the alignment of the curtains, which shows irregularities and some disregard of the right angle; the enclosure in its present empty condition measures a hundred and ten feet from north to south by sixty-seven feet transversely, including wall-thicknesses of from six to eight feet at ground-floor level. The whole curtain is surrounded by a broad plinth, variations in the style of which help to differentiate the structural phases. No evidence of outworks has been found.

The internal arrangements of the remodelled and enlarged castle are described at length, with detailed architectural evidence, in the Inventory of the Ancient Monuments of Kintyre, and no more than an outline of their principal features would be in place in the present work. On this basis, the following points may be made.

The west curtain runs south from the south-west corner of the former hall-house, a garderobe-tower projecting from it at the junction. It is pierced, at first-floor level, by four crosslet loops set in wide embrasures; but details of arrangements on the floor above are hidden by a strip of concrete laid along the wall-head for protection. The three embrasures to the north opened off a timber gallery, and the southernmost one from a room at the west end of the south range. The gallery communicated at its north end with the first-floor room of the hall-house, and also with the garderobe-tower. This latter, which had another door at ground level, was three storeys in height; and though the internal fittings were all removed when the tower was adapted as a dovecot, it can still be seen how the chutes were arranged in echelon from front to back at the successively higher levels.

The south range, at ground level, incorporates the old chapel in the manner already described, and must have been traversed by a pend leading in from the gatehouse. The line of the range is continued by the south-east tower, which projects east from the south-east corner of the enceinte; and this is likely to have contained some domestic offices at ground level as its south wall is pierced by an inlet for water, formerly provided externally with a stone basin. The hall occupied the first floor of the south range east of the gatehouse together with the adjoining part of the south-east tower; it was about fifty feet long by twenty feet wide, and was lit on the south by three embrasured slit-windows and on the east and north respectively by two more, these last and one of the southerly windows being in the tower-projection. The fireplace may have been in the vanished north wall, as well, probably, as an entrance reached by an outside stair. West of the hall there was a room from which access was obtained to the portcullis chamber in the gatehouse. The top of the south wall shows the remains of a series of embrasured openings, which also continue round the south and east sides of the south-east tower; these compare with openings in the top floor of the latrine tower, and probably represent a low upper floor above the hall. A similar arrangement no doubt continued along the top of the west curtain.

The gatehouse projects two feet from the face of the south curtain, and contains the entrance-gate with the portcullis chamber above it. The outermost arch has lost its red-sandstone voussoirs, which have been replaced in rubble; inside this there is a slot through which attackers could have been assailed from above, and then two more arches with a slot for the portcullis between them. On the inner side of the innermost arch there was hung a double-leaved door, secured by a sliding bar of which the socket-hole can still be seen. The portcullis chamber has been walled off to form a dovecot, and its two south-facing crosslet loops have been partially destroyed by the insertion between them of a pigeon-port. Two others are placed in the re-entrant angles of the gatehouse so as to command the face of the curtain to either side.

Next to be considered are the east curtain-wall and the north-east corner of the enceinte, with the small latrine tower that projects northwards at the angle. In the original arrangement, a range of buildings occupied the corner and extended southwards for about fifty-five feet; this was divided by a partition wall now represented by the south wall of the lower part of the tower. Today, however, only the part north of the partition remains, as the rest was removed in the sixteenth century; and with it went the original access to the first floor of the north part, with the result that a forestair, as at present, had to be provided instead. The upper part of the east curtain was likewise rebuilt, with rubble merlons lacking red-sandstone dressings. Traces of the vanished portion of the east range may be seen, though altered, in the postern door and the entrance to the tower's ground-floor room, both under the forestair, and in the window at the stair's head. The ground-floor room shows remains of two original windows, one, on the east, blocked by the insertion of a sixteenth-century barrel vault and the other, on the north, altered by the insertion of a horizontal gun port of a date late in that century. The west wall, which is actually the east wall of the hall-house, retains the latter's plinth. In the first-floor room the east and north windows are original, though the latter, like the garderobe in the corner, has undergone alterations; the south window was converted from a fireplace when the building to the south was demolished. Access to the wall-head, or, after the sixteenth-century alterations, to the upper floors, was by the straight stair in the thickness of the east curtain.

Reference has been made more than once to alterations made early in the sixteenth century, and these call for a word of comment. Until the end of the fifteenth century Skipness seems to have remained with the Macdonalds, but in 1495, after the final forfeiture of the Lord of the Isles, the lordship was granted to Sir Duncan Forestare, the King's Comptroller, presumably as a step in the absorption of the Isles' dominions into the kingdom as a whole. Shortly afterwards, James IV began to build up a Campbell regime in the west, and in 1502 Skipness was granted to the 2nd Earl of Argyll; in 1511 it was passed to his son Archibald, and thereafter it remained in Campbell hands until 1843. It is natural to connect new building with new proprietors, and the work done at the beginning of the sixteenth century may therefore be attributed with confidence to the new Campbell lords. In accordance with the fashion of the time, the building took the form of a tower-house, rising in the north-east corner of the enclosure in the manner already described. It added two storeys to the height of the thirteenth-century structure, with a turnpike stair for access, and adapted the garderobe-tower. The rooms contain many minor architectural features, the significance of which is discussed by the Ancient Monuments Commissioners; one on the outer face of the north wall is easily seen – a pair of built-up crenelles of the old parapet-walk, with the merlon between them pierced by a crosslet loop.

The final phase in the evolution of the tower-house came later in the sixteenth century, and entailed the construction, or reconstruction, of a garret above the third-floor room; a cap house, provided with a fireplace and garderobe, at the head of the turnpike stair; and a corbelled-out parapet-walk surrounding the top of the tower. The gun loop in the ground-floor room (*supra*) is no doubt to be associated with the rest of this new work. These improvements appear to be too early to be connected with the Civil War, though some work of repair and improvement was probably done after 1642, when Matthew Campbell undertook to 'sufficientlie Beit and repaire the tower of the said castell of Skipneis in the roofe, loftis, doores, windowes and all other necessares'. In 1645 Alastair MacDonald, son of Coll Ciotach, having deserted Montrose's army after the battle of Kilsyth in order to wage a private war on Argyll, invaded Kintyre and worked fearful destruction; at this time the Castle sustained a 'long and hard seidge' and was reduced to 'extraordinar distres' before it was relieved. The defender, Malcom MacNachtan of Dundarawe, never recovered from the hardships that he underwent. After Argyll's rebellion of 1685, an order was made for the 'razeing doun' of the Castle, as the laird, Walter Campbell, had been involved along with his chief; however, he made a petition to the Privy Council, stating that he proposed to leave the Castle and go to live in Bute, and the building was accordingly spared.

The farm buildings that my father removed were partly inside the curtain-wall and partly outside on the east, where they formed a second courtyard. As far as my memory serves, a range containing a large barn ran along the inner side of the south curtain; the main entrance was partly filled up, but housed a side-door into the barn which, with another opening opposite into the court, provided the cross-draught required for winnowing by hand. Another range, with stables for the farm horses, occupied the inner side of the west curtain as far as the pigeon tower; the first floor of the south-east tower contained the estate carpenter's workshop; and the ground floor of the main tower was a store for bulky material. Before separate stables were built about 1883 (p.89), stabling for the carriage horses, with the coachman's house, stood in the north-east corner of the enclosure. The main tower had been pointed, and had been given a new roof, floors and stair, by my father long before my time; it was uninhabited, but the first-floor room was used for concerts, tenants' dances and other public functions.

The outer yard was entered at its north-west corner, and comprised three ranges of buildings with the midden in the centre. On the west were byres, backed against the face of the curtain-wall; on the south a range, probably of further byres, which carried imitation battlements on its back wall; and on the north pig styes. The east side was closed by the back of a sawmill shed, open on the east towards a woodyard; the circular saw was driven by a massive steam engine of very moderate power. Outside the yard, to the north of the pig styes, there stood a large hayshed of galvanised iron, inhabited by a distinctive race of cats – smaller than ordinary cats, light grey in colour with stripes, and having ear-tips slightly bent over. They were excessively wild and unfriendly. Like the so-called Alloa cats, ultimately descended from a known Russian ship's cat whose vessel put in for repairs and was laid up in the port for months, they may well have originated from a single visiting tom.

Across the road from the woodyard stood the dairy, built by my grandmother to supply the House with milk, butter and eggs. Though carrying a stock to compare with a comfortable croft, it was independent of the Home Farm and was run by my mother through the agency of a dairymaid-henwife. The plan of the building would not have passed muster today on hygienic grounds, as the milk-room and dairymaid's bedroom opened right and left off a short entrance lobby which led straight into the byre; while beyond the byre were two rooms given over to the hens, with nests for sitting on eggs, and the midden was just behind. But in fact the milk-room looked delightfully clean and fresh, with a stone-flagged floor and great shining tin pans of milk set out on shelves of grey slate. The churn, admittedly, was wooden, and took the form of a barrel mounted horizontally which rotated as a handle was cranked. An older, obsolete, churn stood in the corner of the room – an upright, conical affair, agitated by a kind of piston.

The Castle has naturally attracted a certain amount of folklore. One story, told to my mother, concerned the arrival of the first contingent of Campbells. The garrison was naturally unwilling to leave, but the Campbells induced them to come out of the Castle for a conference. As a friendly gesture they organised a picnic on a certain small rocky knoll a short distance east of the chapel; its top looks conveniently flat, though this may be due to quarrying in the nineteenth century for material to build a stone dyke. They provided ample liquor, and this proved so potent that the guests all went to sleep on the spot when the party was over, and the Campbells were thus able to enter the Castle without opposition. The knoll has a Gaelic name, translated for my mother's benefit as 'The Hill of the Wine'.

A laird's heroine-wife has been recorded by Mrs Higginson, and the story can best be given in her own words. 'This lady', she writes,

> was wife of Colin first laird Campbell of Skipness he was killed at Edinburgh some said it was a hanging matter for treason at any rate he died in Edinburgh she was a widow when she married Colin Campbell her former husband being the laird of Dunardrigh. She was often called the Lady of Dunardrigh, but oftener Big Lady Ann of Skipness. She was over six feet in height and very strong. She had for supper a bowl of brose made of oatmeal and marrow every night she spoke Gaelic better than English. One day in her time the door of the castle facing the house was out of order it took seven men to lift it down off its hinges. When it was mended the seven men was trying to lift the door on to its hinges again, they could not manage it. Lady Ann was passing at the time and seeing their distress she told them to keep out of her way, she took hold of the door herself and lifted it up bodily and put it on its hinges herself. Another time a poor tramp came to the House. Lady Ann told the servants to give the tramp her bowl of brose with the marrow in it and to give him a bed in the barn for the night. The brose was too strong for the tramp it nearly killed him it was said that he was swollen as tight as a drum and they had to be rolling him about all night on straw.

Lady Ann does not shape well as an historical figure. Two lairds with wives called Ann are recorded by Burke, one of them having had two, respectively in his first and third marriages, but none of the three women corresponds at all closely with Mrs Higginson's picture. The earlier of the lairds in question was Walter, 5th of Skipness, who married, first Ann, daughter of Stewart of Ardvorlich and widow of Macdonald of Sand,* and, third, another Ann Stewart, daughter of Sir James Stewart of Bute. This Walter died about 1702. The other was his grandson Colin (p.48), who married his cousin Ann, daughter of Daniel Campbell of Shawfield and died in 1756. Neither of these husbands was 'killed in Edinburgh', and, though the first Campbell laird, Mrs Higginson's choice, did in fact suffer that fate, his name was Archibald, not Colin, and his wife, though previously a widow, was not Ann but Jean and her first husband had been not MacTavish of Dunardary but the Earl of Glamis. She was, in fact, the unhappy Lady Glamis who was burnt for treason in 1536 and later declared innocent. Ann Campbell of Shawfield, again, would seem to be rather out of character, coming as she did of a 'detribalised' family with big business interests in Glasgow; but the fact that she presented the parish with fine Communion plate (p.49) suggests that she was a considerable local personage, and as her husband was called Colin she may be the likeliest candidate. In any case, whoever she was, Big Ann must somehow have assimilated at least two pieces of extraneous folklore. One of them evidently derives from the dramatic death of Lady Glamis' husband Archibald, who crashed down the rocks at Edinburgh Castle while making his escape out of prison. As the Privy Council records the affair, 'the said umquhile Archibald enforcit himself to brek oure said ward and tharethrow deceist haistelie'. The other probably refers to the supposed hanging, in 1689, of John MacTavish, 7th of

* G. Harvey Johnston (*The Heraldry of the Campbells*, 19) ignores this lady, crediting the 5th Laird with two wives only.

Dunardary, which in fact never took place, as he died normally in 1677.

The *gruagach*,* in my childhood, was almost more than folklore. She was credited with living in the ground-floor room of the south-east tower, and some of the men about the farm were probably inclined to avoid that part of the establishment after dark. Mrs Higginson may be right in saying that she came and left with the Campbells, but something of her influence seems nevertheless to have survived. An extract from Mrs Higginson's account of her is worth quoting verbatim:

> There is not the slightest doubt that there was such a creature in the castle at that time. There was a woman living in a room at the castle who looked after the hens, etc. She was a widow named Mrs Barton this Mrs Barton used to tell how the green lady used to help her feed the hens in the evening, always in the evening or at night she was never seen till after sunset she used to put her head on Mrs Barton's knee and get her hair combed.

Mrs Higginson states elsewhere that she had beautiful golden hair, and for that matter a great head of hair seems to have been the hallmark of a *gruagach*:

> she was very small just like a child in stature she wore a green silk dress. She had neither shoes nor stockings on she would help Mrs Barton to tidy up her house. When the Campbells would be away from home, a night or two before they returned the green lady would be working in the house setting it in order for their home coming. Whether the servants had word of the Campbells coming or not when they heard the green lady working they knew the Campbells were not far off. The Campbells were in the habit of giving a ball at New Year time. At one of these balls a brother of Mrs Barton attended to help the servants but early in the evening he felt unwell and he went to bed in Mrs Barton's room every one seems to have been so busy no one looked near him until the ball was over and

---

* Lacking Gaelic, we heard and adopted this word, no doubt quite wrongly, as if it was *gruach*, without the 'ag' in the middle.

then he was found nearly dead in bed. The green lady nearly killed him for being in Mrs Barton's bed she was boxing him all night they took him away to his home in Lochranza. He never recovered from the thrashing the green lady gave him he died very shortly after.

It may or may not have been this Green Lady that was once seen by my sister Mrs Vaughan Johnson. The latter had taken her small daughter into the first-floor room in the tower, when she noticed a face looking round the left-hand jamb of the door. It was placed as if the owner was standing on the bottom step of the stair just outside, and peering into the room to see the child. Nobody, in fact, was there.

7. THE CHAPEL AND THE CHURCHES

It was shown in the last chapter how St Columba's chapel, owned by the monks of Paisley, became incorporated in the fabric of the Castle when this was enlarged at the end of the thirteenth century. The chapel of St Brendan, which stands near the eastern end of Skipness Bay some three hundred and fifty yards south-east of the Castle, is dated by the experts to the turn of the thirteenth and fourteenth centuries, and shows certain features which lead them to believe that it was built by the same group of masons as worked on the enlargement of the Castle. It is therefore natural to connect the two events, and to suppose that St Brendan's was built for the Paisley monks in compensation for the loss of St Columba's.

The chapel, now roofless, is a single-chambered building eighty-two feet long by twenty-seven feet wide, including wall-thicknesses of up to four feet and a half. It is built of grey schist rubble, perhaps quarried close by in the Chapel Wood, with red-sandstone dressings like those in the Castle. A plinth runs all round the base of the walls. The main entrance-door was in the south wall of the nave, with a smaller doorway on the north; a chancel doorway has been blocked by a wall-monument outside. The east gable, of which the red-sandstone skews are well cut and in good preservation, contains a window divided into two pointed lights by a central mullion, above the branched top of which there is a small lozenge-shaped light. The other windows are all single lancets apart from a small square-headed one on the west gable; this presumably lighted a loft, the floor of which could have rested

46

on the scarcement seen on the face of the gable. The remains
of a bellcote stand on the gable-head.

The graveyard contains five late-mediaeval slabs, all illustrated in White's *Kintyre*, and in the later K.A. Steer and
J.W.M. Bannerman, *Late Medieval Monumental Sculpture in
the West Highlands* (Royal Commission on the Ancient and
Historical Monuments of Scotland, 1977). Four, dating from
between the late fourteenth and early sixteenth centuries, bear
respectively

(a) a Crucifixion, with SS Mary and John; a man with a
    spear and a woman with a rosary, each in a niche; and
    a stag pursued by a hound;
(b) foliaceous cross; a sword with depressed quillons, and an
    oviform pommel with a tang button; interlaced foliage
    and a plain tablet;
(c) leaves and stems forming a cross and two circles, with
    three blank panels below as if for inscriptions;
(d) a sword.

A fifth slab, of the early sixteenth century, is in the style of
Dr Steer's Loch Awe school; it carries a niche, crowned by
a pair of dragons' heads, which contains a man armed with a
spear and a sword and wearing a conical helmet. In its lower
half interlaced foliage terminates in twin beasts, at either end,
and below this is a hound pursuing a stag.

The series of post-Reformation headstones begins, in so far
as their dates are legible, in 1721. Few stones show emblems
or epitaphs of particular interest, though Donald Kaymand,
tailor in Colphen (1727), is given his scissors and 'goose', and
William Ferreor, gardener in Skipness (1727 and 1737), has
appropriate gardening tools. A stone commemorating Angus
McKinnin in Sron (Strone), who died in 1737, shows a
man ploughing with four horses; and of him Mrs Higginson
records that he was ploughing a field on Caolfin near the lip
of the scars, and was dragged over and killed when his team
stampeded. This, however, is pretty certainly an aetiological
myth, as the same scene not only recurs in several other
Kintyre graveyards but is also known in Ayrshire – whence,

in fact, the design, if not the stone itself, may well have been imported. A wall-monument in the Campbell enclosure commemorates Colin Campbell, Captain of Skipness, who died in 1756. He was the seventh Campbell laird, and served with distinction in the 'Forty-five, particularly as commander of the garrisons of Kilchurn and Mingary Castles. The other wall-monument in this enclosure commemorates Robert Campbell, the tenth laird, who died in 1814 and was buried at Bothwell. The headstone is that of his infant daughter Gabrielle (1812).

Mrs Higginson records that the graveyard used to suffer from body-snatching, being conveniently close to the shore for raids by boat at night. The last case of which she knew occurred about 1810. She states that a certain family, whose name she is careful to withhold for the sake of surviving descendants, was believed to trade by sea in corpses from Skipness and other local graveyards, making use of a 'wherry', a decked, two-masted craft.

No record has been found of when the Chapel was last used for worship, but this can hardly have been before 1692, as a minister is recorded under that date as having been translated to Craignish parish 'from the united parishes of Kilcalmonell and Kilberry and the chapel of Skipness'. The building may, in fact, have continued in use until a new church was built at Claonaig in 1756, though the *Statistical Account of Scotland* says nothing about it in describing the reorganisation of the parishes effected in 1753. A possible hint as to the arrangements obtaining after the Reformation, but presumably before the reorganisation of the parish in 1753, may be provided by the name Cnocan Tigh Searmonaich, given on the OS map of 1867 to a hillock about a quarter of a mile west-south-west of Glenreasdell Mains. Professor Jackson informs me that this name, though ungrammatical, must be intended to mean 'the hillock of the house of the preacher', which in turn suggests that local pastoral duty was at some time in the hands of a lay preacher.

The late Donald Macarthur, a former Session Clerk, once

told me that before a church was built at Claonaig services were held in a building near the east end of Claonaig Bay; no traces of this are visible today, though some foundations can be seen about a hundred and seventy yards north-east of the point where the B8001 curves away from the shore. The OS map of 1867 marks the site of a burial-ground on the south side of Claonaig Glen, of which a tradition survived until Captain White's time though no physical traces remain. Its rather solitary position on a hillside tends to recall John Knox's advice in the First Book of Discipline, that burials should be in some 'secret and convenient place, lying in the most free air'. Donald Macarthur further informed me that there had been a cemetery for shipwrecked sailors and unbaptised infants at the point marked 'Flagstaff' in Claonaig Bay; this may possibly be the burial-ground named Leachd na Gall by Mrs Higginson, and placed by her on the shore below Auchnastrone. She mentions, in addition, An Reilig, on the shore near the Oragaig Burn, and Goirtcan an t'Saighdear, in the Larachmor region.

Claonaig Church is a very plain, harled structure with three pointed windows in each side, an empty bellcote on its west gable-head, and a small session-house at its west end. Its general appearance suggests a date in the early nineteenth century, and it may represent a reconstruction of the church of 1756 though no record of rebuilding exists. It was noted as needing repair in 1843, and I have heard that my grandmother had work done on it after 1866. Further work is recorded in 1892.

The older items of the Communion plate are (i) a pair of silver cups, of twenty ounces each, made by Ker and Dempster of Edinburgh in 1764. They are inscribed 'To the Church of Clenag given by Ann Campbell, Lady of Skipness', and bear the date 1765 and a heraldic assemblage derived from the arms of Campbell of Skipness. This consists of a heart-shaped object with a ragged border, charged with a gyronny of eight and surrounded by eight crescents; there is also floreate mantling and, on a wreath, a pair of crossed oars as a crest. Above is the motto 'Terra marique fide'. A silver flagon, likewise dated 1765, is noted in the parish record as having disappeared by 1943. (ii) An undated pewter cup inscribed 'For the Paroch of Saddell and Cardell'. (iii) An undated pewter flagon inscribed 'For the United Parishes of Skipness and Saddal'.

The whole of the combined parish of Saddell and Skipness was under a single minister until 1872, when Skipness was disjoined as a *quoad sacra* parish and received a minister of its own, who lived in the village. From 1892 to 1906 the incumbent was the Rev. John Maclachlan, who retired from active duty in the latter year for reasons of health but retained the nominal appointment, with the result that, until his death in 1930, subsequent ministers had to rank as assistants. The Rev. Duncan MacNaughton occupied the post from 1906 to 1908, and the Rev. John M. Menzies from 1908 to 1913. Services were held in both Gaelic and English, the Gaelic ones becoming less frequent as the use of the language faded, and ceasing in 1949. Music was supplied by a precentor, Neil Currie the innkeeper, who obtained his key with a tuning-fork. A thatched cottage stood immediately south of the church, and this had been a school until about 1868.

Claonaig was thus a kind of parochial centre, the Established Church having no place of worship in Skipness village before 1898, when the mission-church of St Brendan was opened; this was built by private subscription to the design of my brother-in-law, Bertram Vaughan Johnson, and my father placed in it, in memory of his mother, a stained-glass window designed by himself in the style of the mediaeval West Highland sculptures of which he had made a study. It bears the legend 'In memoriam Susannae Roope Graham matris dilectissimae filius'. The foundation stone was laid ceremonially by my mother in 1896, the silver trowel and ornamental mallet that she used being now among the possessions of the Church. The former is inscribed 'Presented to Mrs Graham of Skipness on the occasion of her laying the Memorial stone of St Brendan's Church, Skipness, 30th May, 1896'; the latter has a silver inlay inscribed 'Presented by William Cook (wright)'. The font is of later origin. It is in the form of a large silver quaich, of twenty ounces, bearing the Sheffield mark of 1938 and inscribed 'Presented to St Brendan's Church, Skipness, to the Glory of God and in grateful thanks for the Baptism of Simon Audouin Oakes, September 11th, 1937'; its wooden case bears, in addition, the words 'The first Baptism to take place in this Church'.*

I remember the building of this church very clearly, and particularly the matter of the foundation stone. A cavity was cut in the stone, and my father put in to this, for the benefit of future archaeologists, a sealed-up marmalade-pot containing some contemporary coins and a copy of the *Glasgow Herald*. I also remember that at four years old I was fascinated by the process of melting pitch and sealing the pot's canvas cover.

A Free Church, now the village hall, was built in 1892.

From a rubbing made by Mr G.E.S. Dunlop of the heraldic design on the Skipness Communion Cup referred to on page 49. The arms are those of the donatrix' husband, differenced from the Campbell gyronny, for him by the indented bordure of a sixth son, charged with eight of a second son's crescents, and for her as his wife in couverture, by the outlines of the shield and bordure being curved, and floriated, while his motto appears on a scroll with ribbons. (Ref: A.C. Fox-Davies, *A Complete Guide to Heraldry*. Edinburgh 1929, pp.139, 469, 503, 579.)

* *Footnote*: In July 1980 Angus Graham's ashes rested here, having been brought from Edinburgh to be interred in the nineteenth-century extension of the graveyard of the medieval Chapel, after which a commemorative gathering was held in this building.

Joanna Gordon

8. THE VILLAGE

The linear lay-out of Skipness today took shape when the village was traversed after 1756 by an extension of the High Road from the parochial centre at Claonaig (p.18). Evidence from early maps and local tradition suggest that no part of the village was ever a 'castleton' comparable to those removed from close proximity to many lairds' residences in Argyll, as elsewhere, in the course of 'improvements'. The earliest of the maps, in Blaeu's *Theatrum Orbis Terrarum*, 1654, marks 'Skibbenes' on two different plates, those of 'Cantyra' and 'Arania'; both acknowledge Pont as their source, and their correspondence with Robert Gordon's MS map of Kintyre, itself no doubt based on Pont's field work, is very close. In each case Blaeu makes use of his usual symbol of a building with a high spire, and although one of these symbols is placed west of the mouth of the burn, i.e. in a position colourably corresponding with that of the present village, the addition of the name 'Chailfein' shows that the symbol refers to a farm of Caolfin, which was probably, then as now, well up on the hill behind. On the 'Cantyra' map, no fewer than three of these symbols are grouped on the east side of the burn, and relate to the Castle.

Roy's map was surveyed in the 1740s and '50s, and shows that until the High Road linked Skipness with Claonaig, a track from Glenreasdell (p.16) slanted down across the slope behind the village, probably crossing the large burn above the island. This area, An-t-Uchd, the breast of the hill, was, according to local tradition, occupied by crofters. A Rent Book of 1836 was edited in 1906, when a note was made that fifty to sixty families had lived upon this ground. William Fraser, the elder, 1843 (p.xvii) got the blame for evicting them, but the names of their houses, as recorded in 1906, suggest that the extension of the High Road along the shore began to attract settlement down to its present line before this time. Tigh-na-drochaid, the Bridge House, for instance, must have been near the earlier of the two bridges shown on the 1867 OS map. This crossed the large burn near the head of the tide, about 120 yards upstream from a ford and stepping-stones which continued in use until the burn broke out its present mouth. Tighean-na-Vuillin, the Mill Houses, were on the far side of this bridge, where marks in parched grass still show up in very dry seasons. Roy's map shows five dots and the word Mill quite correctly in this same' field, though placing Caolfin incorrectly, also on the east side of the burn.

In the years between the arrival of the High Road from Claonaig and the Fraser 'improvements' of the 1840s Skipness village grew up along the shoreline. It is unfortunate that in the only map surviving from near the turn of the century (Langlands 1801) the basic topography is wrong, as it shows the small burn running into the large one instead of into the sea. It marks the road from Claonaig following the present line of the village street though without any houses except four small crofts at the north-east end. The road stops here on reaching the bank of the burn, in the area traditionally named Strathbuie from the yellow broom of the burnside. The highway bridge had apparently not yet been constructed. Mrs Campbell, however, implies its existence in 1813. Thomson's Atlas (No.17) of 1824 is in general agreement with Langlands, though correcting his mistake about the confluence of the burns.

In 1833, still ten years before William Fraser, William Dobie, in his 'Perambulations in Kintyre', described the village as 'a long row of thatched houses, with one or two detached, like sentinels, at each of its extremities'. The western 'sentinels' may have been the houses near the sea-pool, where the big burn in its old course captured the outfall of the Crow Glen burn before turning south and out into the sea in the corner of the bay. Tigh-na-Craoibhe is the name of this settlement shown on the 1867 OS map with all but one of its houses lying between the shore and the High Road immediately west of its bridge over the Crow Glen burn. These were most likely fishermen's dwellings. Four or five smacks were worked out of the sea-pool as late as the 1890s, and there is an earlier record of boat-building at this site.

The main part of Dobie's row was probably near the ford and the old bridge, where he mentions a school and an inn immediately east of the point at which the Caolfin farm road now branches off. The ford and the bridge led onto the storm beach between the burn and the sea. Along the crest of this beach a track connected the village with the Mill Field and its houses, the Mansion House, the Castle and, most importantly in earlier times, the Chapel. The importance of that route, in the time before the highway bridge crossed the burn above Strathbuie, made this area a natural focus of development. Even in very early times, settlement was most likely to have taken place here, at the head of the tide, in addition to whatever use was made of the sea-pools. Dobie's eastern 'sentinel' was probably the smithy. This, and three houses nearby, were the only buildings marked on the 1867 OS map at the north-east end of the village, in Strathbuie. From this map it appears that the village of even so late a date as 1867 must have differed considerably from what we see today, but the village as I first remember it was very much the same as at present. After 1866, my grandmother and my father carried out a great programme of building and improvement, largely responsible for the appearance of Skipness village now. Most of the houses were occupied by employees of the estate. Strathbuie contained, on its north-west side, three large double houses and one small one, the last a survival from before the Ordnance survey of 1867 and the others all built new by my grandmother or father. St Brendan's Church was not built until 1896-98, as has been described on p.50. It is interesting to recall that box-beds, now regarded as fair game by amateurs of vernacular building, were still being installed as ordinary pieces of equipment in some, at least, of the nineteenth-century houses. About the centre of Strathbuie there was a small general shop, kept by Margaret Mackinlay. Before her marriage to Ronald Mackinlay, a shoemaker, crippled by a club foot, she had been my mother's head housemaid, but I remember her only in her capacity as 'General Merchant', with Ronald conducting his affairs in an outhouse beside the shop. Ronald, of course, was not a mere cobbler and botcher, but one of those craftsmen, now extinct, who made shoes and boots from the sheet of leather onwards. Margaret's approach to work was likewise old-fashioned; once, when entreated by my mother to take things rather more easily, she is said to have replied, 'When I see my duties before me, I canna rest!'

The smithy, which stood at the curve of the road, has been removed of recent years, while the house which in 1867 still faced it from the opposite side of the road disappeared earlier. This house was probably associated with the smithy, as the field in which it stood, between the road and the burn, was officially 'the smith's pendicle'. The smithy was a thrilling place for a small boy, with its little volcano of finely broken coal in the middle of the hearth, and the great bellows with a Highland cow's horn on the end of the blowing handle; but in fact it was no doubt exactly like other smithies, and calls for no particular notice.

In the western part of the village, the double house next the smithy is new since 1867, and so are the outhouse beside the post-office, the school and the village hall. The house next the school is older than Ordnance survey, and so is the one next to the Caolfin road-end; this latter being marked 'School' on the map of 1867. A house has disappeared from immediately east of the road-end, and so has the group in and near the bottom of the Crow Glen, though the last of these was occupied until about 1897. The remaining houses may or may not be reconstructions. The school bears the date 1868, in which year the Claonaig school was moved to Sperasaig. The schoolmaster, Thomas Johnstone, was highly regarded as a teacher, but his politics, which were those of the fervent Clydeside Reds, may sometimes have appeared unfortunate in a quiet West Highland backwater. The outhouse east of the post-office was formerly a bakery, but baking had stopped before my time though the widow of the last baker still managed the post-office.

The post-office contained a telegraph instrument which ranks in my memory almost with the smithy fire, and would probably qualify today for a place in a science museum. It had a large dial with letters arranged round the circumference, and in sending a message the operator spelt it out by pressing the appropriate buttons while generating the necessary current by turning a handle. Incoming messages she read off by watching a needle flick from letter to letter. A thoroughly West Highland process known as 'talking over the wires' could sometimes save the cost of an actual telegram if the subject at issue happened to be within the knowledge of the operator at the other end. (For that matter, I confess to having once worked this oracle, between Edinburgh and Quebec, on a Saturday afternoon when the cable-office was slack.) Local telegrams were delivered by an old Irishman called John Devlin, believed to be a retired soldier but notable for his precise and formal speech, who lived in a wooden bothy at the back of the former bakehouse and did a very small trade in mending shoes. The telegraph service was installed in 1876 with an annual guarantee by my father; the extension, however, seems to have been only from Claonaig, as a line passing Claonaig and serving the east coast is marked on the OS map of 1867.

The water-supply was piped from a reservoir and filter in the Crow Glen, and was delivered at two stand-pipes, one at either end of the village. In earlier days, people had dipped their water out of the burn, while also dumping their refuse along its bank, and for this or other reasons cases of diphtheria had occurred. When water and ash-pits were reformed, my mother used to keep a sharp eye on signs of incipient middens along the burnside, and would drop on the guilty woman with telling weight.

Every house in the village had a garden plot in front, but about the year 1905 it occurred to my sister, later Mrs Gordon, that some of the gardens were very poorly kept, and to encourage improvement she organised an annual flower-show. Competition was open to anyone living on the estate, and there were classes not only for flowers and vegetables, but also for such things as butter, cheese, scones, oatcakes, knitting, shepherds' crooks, and the singing of Gaelic songs. This last event was generally won by Peter Campbell, the keeper at Claonaig, whose splendid black beard seemed to give his voice a send-off. I once won a prize myself, for a pair of socks in the under-fourteen knitting. The scheme was a brilliant success, creating enormous interest and bringing out the gardens in a blaze of colour; and the actual shows, which were held in the Castle courtyard and included a formal prize-giving, attracted hordes of visitors. The judging was done by neutral experts from outside; I remember how the ex-Provost of a certain Royal Burgh was invited, as being a profoundly knowledgeable grocer, to judge the cheese and butter, and how he found it necessary to sup a mouthful of whisky between each sample and the next, as they tended to 'vitiate the taste'.

Before leaving the subject of the village, I must add a word about one of its notable inhabitants, namely, the Mrs Higginson to whose collection of local lore I make such frequent reference. Her history is more or less as follows. John Campbell, the Home Farm shepherd,* in his younger days once went over to Arran to help some farmer with his lambing. Some time after his return, a strange woman of rather forbidding aspect walked up the village street carrying a bundle; and having ascertained where John Campbell lived, she deposited the bundle on the doorstep and left without further explanation or contact with any of the neighbours. The bundle proved to contain an infant girl; and although John Campbell was a bachelor, he was fully experienced in

* Not to be confused with John Campbell the ploughman, mentioned on p.97.

caring for orphan lambs, and proceeded without turning a hair to bring the child up in similar way. In this he was entirely successful – she flourished, was trained as a nurse, subsequently married a tailor who worked at Cnocandonn, and after the latter's death came to live with her father in his attic bothy over Margaret Mackinlay's shop. No doubt her father supplied much of the material for her stories, and she could also have picked the brains of a certain old Granny Maclean, who lived in another bothy in the same building. It was this latter old woman, by the way, who told my father the tale about St Columba quoted above on p.16.

9. THE OLD HOUSE

Until it was demolished in 1881, the Old House stood on what later became a lawn immediately in front of its successor, and close to the lip of the bank that crosses the whole breadth of the front garden. No measured drawings exist, but an idea of its size and external appearance can be gained from the small block-plan shown on the 25-inch Ordnance map surveyed in 1867, together with a water-colour sketch apparently made by someone with architectural training, and a few old photographs.

In its final phase, the house was evidently a complex of several periods. The original core was a central block of two storeys and an attic, aligned from east-south-east to west-north-east, with a range of other buildings abutting on either end and running back to form the two sides of a court open to the north-north-east. The whole was harled, and all the roofs were of slate. The central block measured about seventy by twenty-five feet, and had a large, flat-roofed perch or garden-room projecting from the centre of its front. This projection, which had a three-light window on the south and an entrance-door on the east, was no doubt an addition, covering an original doorway in the centre of the façade. The original fenestration was probably symmetrical, with three gables in the attic storey, two large windows on the first floor under the large central gable, and a single window on both the ground and the first floors under the smaller lateral ones. The symmetry, however, had been upset by a tall window east of the central pair, which extended downwards from the first floor into the upper part of the ground floor; this

59

suggests lighting for a stair, inserted in some modification of the original arrangements. The two smaller lateral gables may likewise represent enlargements of original dormer-windows. Gables and gablets were crow-stepped, with ogee skewputs, and a chimney-stack stood on each gable and on the large gable. A shallow corbel-course above the first-floor windows advanced the upper part of the façade a few inches. The north elevation was similar, but had no entrance-door and nothing to correspond with the inserted tall window.

The line of the front was carried eastwards for about thirty feet by a single-storeyed wing, which then returned north for about the same distance. Where this wing abutted on the east end of the central block, its roof-ridge was slightly below the tops of the first-floor windows. Its south side had three large windows, and three or four more openings appear indistinctly in its east side. This structure contained, in its internal angle, the south-eastern corner of the court, which was rounded and contained a window with an oeil-de-boeuf above; abutting on its northern end there was a two-storeyed building with a hipped roof, which presumably extended the total length of the range to the seventy-five feet shown on the block-plan.

The west range seems to have been partially rebuilt between 1867 and 1877, as a photograph of the latter year shows its south end as flush with the façade of the central block while the block-plan, of the former, sets its corner back several feet. In 1877, at any rate, the structure abutting on the west end of the central block was a two-storeyed wing with four ground-floor and two first-floor windows on the south and a narrow first-floor slit on the west. On the west the roof was hipped, and one very tall and one short chimney rose from the western wall-head; the internal corner, again rounded, contained a door and an oeil-de-boeuf. At the north end of the wing there was another door and a chimney-stack. According to the block-plan, this wing was again about seventy-five feet long overall, the courtyard between the wings being some ninety feet wide by fifty deep.

The interior of the house is known to have been very

awkwardly arranged; for example, the only access from the guests' bedrooms to the bathroom was through the drawing-room. It was felt that the difficulties could not be overcome by further alterations, my father and grandmother having already made some though no details of them are on record; and my parents were the readier to rebuild as an alarming scream, not traceable to any human agency, made itself heard in the house from time to time.

Very little can be said about the origin and growth of the house. The late Hon. Mrs Scott of Harden, in studying the history of her ancestors, the Campbells of Skipness, obtained the date 1706 for its building from some source which cannot now be identified; and this date agrees with a tradition, likewise derived from Mrs Scott, that the laird's family lived for a time at Culindrach after the Castle was abandoned. On other evidence this last event has been dated tentatively to about 1685 (p.40). Mr J.G. Dunbar has informed me that the central block conforms fully with the standards and fashions at the beginning of the eighteenth century, though he is surprised to find this example in the comparatively backward West Highlands. It is perhaps allowable to suspect a connection between the building of the wings and some injection of money from the Shawfield branch of the family; this might well have occurred either when Colin, the seventh laird, married the daughter of Daniel Campbell of Shawfield and Islay, or when the estate passed, on Colin's death in 1756, to Daniel's younger brother John. The later date would agree better than the earlier with Dobie's statement that the house was built 'some sixty years' before his visit in 1833; this is plainly wrong as it stands, but might be true of additions made in, say, the 1760s or '70s. It is true that Langlands' map of 1801 shows a house which, though drawn to a very small scale, consists only of a block without wings; but this is unlikely to be an accurate representation as no garden enclosure is shown, and a garden certainly existed at least as early as 1727 as a gardener's tombstone of that date still stands in the graveyard (p.47). When Mrs Robert Campbell first visited the place, in 1806, she found the house 'much out of repair', and occupied by a farmer. A modest reminder of older arrangements survives in the form of a well, covered by a stone-built housing, on the right bank of the small burn some thirty yards distant from the House. It was probably intended to supply water for drinking, naturally filtered.

A romantic story, for once not folklore, attaches to the building of the Old House, in that the youngest of the then laird's numerous daughters, still in her early teens, married the master-mason. This is less improbable than it sounds, as before class-prejudice had crystallised in its modern form the younger sons of impoverished lairds were quite commonly apprenticed to trades, and this rather similar action in the case of a daughter would no doubt have been natural enough. The couple were set up in a house at Lagan Geoidh (p.6), and the wife found life so dull in that solitary place that she occupied herself with pole-jumping, to and fro, across the burn. The mason's name was Wilson, and their descendants lived in Skipness until recent years, the last resident member of the family having been the late Mrs Neil Maclachlan. I remember the late Bishop of Glasgow, son of the last Campbell laird, regularly calling on his cousin, Wilson the shoemaker, whenever he came to Skipness.

10. THE HOUSE OF 1881

The Old House, as has been said, suffered from such serious drawbacks that my parents decided to build something new for themselves. Their new house, finished in 1881 and tragically burned in 1969, was sited immediately behind the main block of the old one, and a contemporary photograph, taken from the north-east before the latter was demolished, shows its south-east wing enclosing the south-east end of the new building, apparently just completed. In his design the architect, John Honeyman of Glasgow, seems to have been concerned to tell a kind of fairy-tale of age-long growth, as he combined in the structure a large hall, with two four-light stained-glass windows of vaguely mediaeval aspect, a fairly *vraisemblable* reproduction of a Scottish tower-house with a turnpike stair in a turret, and a range of public rooms and family bedrooms inspired by notions ultimately deriving from Italy. The masonry, too, was made to strengthen the mediaeval illusion, as it matched that of the Castle in the use of grey schist with red-sandstone dressings; the stair-turret, in particular, was all of cut red-sandstone as well as the pepperpot rounds and the great bow-window in the drawing-room. Tucked away at the north-east end was a large courtyard, and the offices and servants' quarters that this kind of establishment needed. The whole certainly bore out the saying that all sorts of liberties can be taken with a Gothic building, whereas a Classical style demands the closest adherence to sets of mathematical rules.

The front door, in the base of the 'tower-house', was round-headed and heavily moulded, and above it was a panel bearing my parents' initials and the date 1881. This assemblage was all in red-sandstone. The door opened into a smallish outer hall, with a chequerboard floor of brown and white marble, dark red walls, and photographic reproductions of Paolo Uccello; and from here one either turned right, into the main hall, or kept straight on into the billiard-room and workshop. There was also a dark-room, and a cloak-room with a pair of lavatories. This part of the house illustrated the deforming effect of habitation by a younger generation, and perhaps also of West Highland influences, on a well-conceived plan, as in my time the hall was housing two motor bicycles, the cushions of the billiard-table had solidified in the damp, salty air, and the table itself was used mainly for fishing-rods, maps and drawings. My father's workshop, too, originally intended for serious work in wood and *repoussé* metal, had become a bear-garden for household repairs and half-baked experimentation.

Whatever might have been thought of its stained-glass windows, the main hall was a splendid place. As one entered, one was faced by the lower flight of a broad wooden stair with corkscrew balusters; this rose under the sills of the windows, turned in the angle of the hall, and rose to first-floor level across the wall at the end. On the end-wall, above the upper flight, was set a large round-topped assemblage of blue tiles, depicting the Baptism of Christ, brought from a garden-house at Xellas, a property of my family's in Portugal. The stair gave, at the top, on to an open gallery, again with corkscrew balusters, which returned along the south side of the hall, giving access to the library and drawing-room, and to the turnpike stair leading to the guests' bedrooms in the tower. Between the end of the gallery and the foot of the turnpike, a small lobby with a rounded projecting front overhung the east end of the hall, in the style of a 'musicians' gallery'; and below it there depended the head of a Highland cow with enormous horns, always known as 'the bull's head' in spite of the horns' patently female character. The lower part of the hall was panelled in dark wood, the south wall being decorated with a collection of weapons; the elaborate fireplace, under the 'bull's head', was lined with Dutch tiles. From the hall, doors opened on the south to the dining and morning-rooms, in the south-east corner to the garden entrance, and in the south-west to the back regions. Beside the stair stood a battery of hot pipes, part of a system of central heating which served the drawing-room and passages. A striking feature of the hall was a set of high-backed Spanish chairs of stamped leather, trimmed with big brass-headed nails.

The hall served a great many useful purposes – family prayers, religious services on Sundays, Christmas-tree functions for school-children, theatricals, dancing, and big sit-down teas when the house was full or callers turned up suddenly. The gallery, however, had a drawback, as a guest coming down to breakfast from a tower bedroom, perhaps whistling, might find himself running the gauntlet, as it were, of the prayers in progress below. Again, it made a glorious speedway for a child longing for a run, but his passage was apt to produce an earthquake in the library as the gallery was borne on ends of the library's floor-joists.

The garden entrance was reached through a heavy swing-door which opened on to its hallway. Here again there was evidence of backsliding from original standards, as big photographs of the Duomo and Campanile at Florence, and a portrait head of my grandmother in white marble, had come to consort with two stuffed animals in glass cases (a badger and an enormous feral tabby-cat), two brass saluting-guns and assorted garden equipment and materials for outdoor games.

The dining room was long enough to hold an expanding table which could seat up to at least seven a side, and besides its door from the hall had a service door which gave access from the kitchen regions. Its windows, one of which was a three-light bay, looked out on the lawn on which the Old House had formerly stood, the bay commanding a field of half a circle. The fireplace was at the east end of the room, and the north and west walls were occupied by singularly unfortunate sideboards. Of the pictures, one was by Neri di Bicci, another by Clouet and another a Gerard Dou, the rest being oil-colour copies of Italian Renaissance originals. The rest of the south-facing range, on the ground floor, contained a bedroom and the schoolroom, with a big window at the end of the passage.

The drawing-room, on the first floor, was long and wide, corresponding with the billiard-room below; it faced east with two large windows and south with one, the angle being occupied by a great round window in a turret. The latter's four lights, of curved plate-glass, were divided by red-sandstone mullions and gave observation for almost three-quarters of a circle; the joints between glass and stone wept copiously in wet weather. The fireplace was in the west wall, and the distinctive features of the room were a grand piano, a grandfather clock, and a large mahogany table with a show of silver. The library, my father's sanctum, was a large comfortable room lined with bookshelves, which looked south over the garden and down the Sound of Kilbrannan. Over the fire hung a copy of Raphael's Madonna del Cardellino.

At the base of the tower stair there was a double bedroom with a dressing-room and lavatory. The stair was of stone, spiralled rather sharply, and gave access to five bedrooms, two on a lower floor and three at the top. None of these rooms was large – my mother, liking large house-parties, had voted at the planning stage for bedrooms to be numerous and small – and one, at the top, was minute; it was also affected by a draught from a doorway leading to a tiny balcony, contrived by the architect as an archaizing touch. There was a lavatory but no bathroom in the tower. The tower was not 'haunted', but when sleeping in it I have heard the noise, not uncommon in Scottish houses, as of a heavy object being bumped down the stair.

The back regions began at the service door of the dining-room, the long tiled passage to the kitchen branching off the one that led to the schoolroom (*supra*). The kitchen passage, which turned left at right angles in the middle, flanked the courtyard on two sides and was lighted from it. On its opposite (right-hand) side there opened, in succession, the stair down to the cellar, my first visit to which I remember clearly, and seeing my initials smoked on the ceiling with a candle; a darkish bedroom pervaded by a curious smell, which might occasionally harbour a piano-tuner detained overnight, or a servant brought by a visitor; the pantry, with an enormous safe for the silver and a telephone to the stables which frequently went out of order – my brother once said, in fact, that it began as a toy and ended up as an incubus; and the store-room, lined all round with shelves and cupboards. Then came the turn to the left, with a china-pantry in a turret which projected at the angle, and beyond the corner, successively, the kitchen and scullery, the cook's bedroom, the servants' hall, an inside larder and a drying-room. The kitchen was conceived on a very generous scale, being a high, almost barn-like, room with a ridged timber roof, set as a kind of wing transversely to the service passage and having three ground-floor windows, and a single small one high up, in its gable-end. To a child it seemed like a cathedral. The whole of one side was given over to a pair of ranges, one large one, which consumed fantastic quantities of coal, and a smaller one which, for some reason, was never used at all. The range heated the water for taps and baths, the hot-water cistern in its lagging being skyed over the kitchen door; the central heating, however, had a separate stove elsewhere, in a room on the courtyard. The other walls were flanked by cupboards and dressers, with big barrels for flour and oatmeal; a service hatch opened on to the passage. The scullery lay beyond the wall that held the ranges, and was entered by a door from the kitchen; however apparently clean, it always seemed to be haunted by an unpleasant sour smell. The distance from the kitchen hatch to the dining-room was about eighteen yards, but the food was run along the passages on a four-wheeled trolley and arrived miraculously hot.

The back door was in a short wing, which branched off southwards opposite the servants' hall and flanked part of the west side of the courtyard. The courtyard was entered by a pend, from which opened the laundry, a large, high room with big windows, a stove specially designed for the heating

of irons, and in the corner by the door a mangle; it was only at
the mangling stage, however, that clothes reached the laundry,
as the washing was done in the wash-house, awkwardly placed,
with its drying-green, some eighty yards away and behind the
garden wall. The laundry-maids carried the clothes to and
fro in enormous two-handled baskets. On to the yard there
gave two open-fronted spaces devoted respectively to coal
and firewood, the latter accommodating also a dog-kennel,
wheel-barrows, ladders, and bulky trash, with a nesting-box
for pigeons in the roof.

The first floor of the back regions was reached by a stair
which rose from opposite the service door of the dining-room;
like the front stair, it had a battery of hot pipes at its foot. On
the landing at its head were nurseries, a bathroom-lavatory
and my mother's bedroom. The balusters along the open side
of the landing were all of iron except for one, a stouter one
on which a gate had once hung; and this, being wooden,
was regularly used by the nursery cat for the purpose of
sharpening her claws. When I visited Skipness in 1966 I
found that it was still in place, half scratched away. Also from
this landing led off the first-floor counterpart of the kitchen
passage. On this were a bedroom or sewing-room, a bathroom
and lavatory and another small bedroom; at the angle of the
passage a housemaid's pantry in a turret, and beyond the angle
a range of servants' bedrooms – two single ones, for the upper
tablemaid and upper housemaid, and the rest double. One of
the rooms in this range served as a linen-room, and there was
also a lumber-room, over the pend that gave entrance to the
courtyard.

The lighting system calls for a short digression. As I first
remember the House, it was lighted by a gas prepared from a
liquid then known as 'gasoline', the outhouse in which the gas
was made being at the safe distance of some seventy yards,
back-to-back with the wash-house. The site was formerly
occupied by the outside lavatory belonging to the Old House.
The generator must have embodied some kind of carburettor,
as I remember massive clockwork which powered a fan; and

in fact the gas-house had had to be built very high to give the weights of the clockwork sufficient fall. In due course this system was superseded by acetylene gas, generated in the usual way from carbide of calcium; and the change brought on a crisis as the acetylene was able to escape through smaller holes than the oil-gas, and the old pipes consequently leaked it out like sieves. A most serious crisis came many years later, when someone melted a gas-pipe inside the House with a plumber's blowtorch and left the raw end open, with the result that an explosive mixture of gas and air formed inside the piping and extended right out to the gas-house; someone else then arrived with a naked light, the mixture in the pipe went off like an instantaneous fuse, and blew the insides out of the gas-machine. Fortunately the relative clause in the insurance policy only relieved the insurers of liability for explosions 'originating within the said gas-house'; and this one, though it did its work within the gas-house, admittedly 'originated' elsewhere. The acetylene gas really gave an admirable light, but was apt to deposit a kind of ash in its burners, which had to be cleaned out with a needle or a fine wire; in the drawing-room it was reinforced by a large oil-lamp, set on a central table, and in the dining-room by candles.

So large a house, so far from facilities for maintenance, was naturally prone to crises. Windows would stick, in an open or closed position, or break their sash-cords; storms would blow slates off the roof, or drive rain in through unsuspected crannies in the walls; while gas, plumbing and bells could go wrong in a variety of ways. Roofing, masonry and woodwork could be dealt with by the estate tradesmen, John McCaig the mason and George Turner the carpenter; but for drains, water and gas it was necessary to summon John MacSporran, the plumber in Tarbert, whose diocese was so large that he was often difficult to come by. This same MacSporran met a tragic end, as he fell from the top of a church-tower in Tarbert. Bells, oddly enough, were in the care of 'Crawford the Butcher', who kept a shop in Tarbert and made weekly visits in his van. He looked after the bells for years, refusing any kind of payment, and at last only accepted a presentation watch when my father showed him the inscription already cut inside. I remember how he taught me to make a primitive chemical battery, keeping the zinc and the carbon carefully apart - 'they daurna tetch'. George Turner enriched our language with an admirable word: to express agreement he habitually said 'eggseggly', so in taxing each other with inaccuracy we would say 'That's not exegg'.

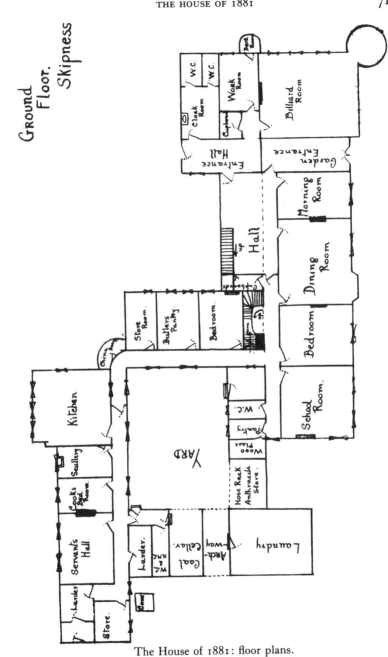

The House of 1881: floor plans.

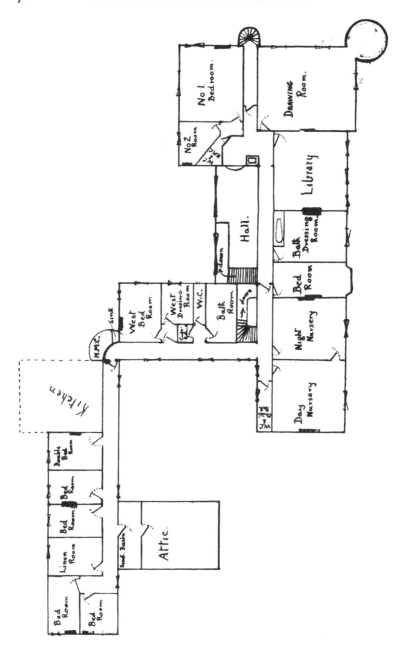

SKIPNESS.

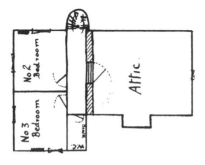

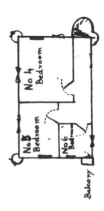

11. LIVING IN THE HOUSE

The pattern of life for which the House was designed now seems as odd as the fantasies that inspired its architect, and a survivor's memories of that pattern may possess a certain interest. An idea of it can be made to emerge from the account of an ordinary day such as might have been lived at the beginning of the twentieth century.

A preliminary point to be considered, however, is the cushion that came between the House and the occupying family – that is to say, the corps of household servants. Exclusive of the nurse, who faded out as the children grew up, and the dairymaid who came in for her meals but sometimes slept at the dairy, the normal complement was nine. At the top were the lady's maid and cook, slightly lower than these three 'uppers' – tablemaid, housemaid and laundrymaid – and down at the bottom their three 'under' counterparts, along with the unhappy kitchen-maid, who devilled for the cook. When the House was full, extras were summoned from the village, for waiting and washing-up; and a skilled seamstress was available in Janet Hyndman, who came in to help the lady's maid with sewing and dress-making. What today seems a miraculously high standard of performance was taken more or less for granted, not least in the dining-room, where Jessie Cameron, the head tablemaid, managed difficult dinners smoothly and coolly, with no dire pauses between one course and the next. The silver never showed a scratch, and I have seen her spacing out the places on the table with a tape. The head housemaid was Christina MacEwan, a great and irrepressible character,

74

and she, with her subaltern, performed prodigies with baths, fires and linen. The tower bedrooms, for example, were far away from any bathroom, and consequently had to be supplied with cans of hot water for hip-baths – and that not only in the morning but at dressing-time too, if necessary, after a day's shooting. And then the baths had to be emptied. There were also fires to be laid, lighted, and cleared out the following morning, and although a man from outside brought coal into the house, and dumped periodical supplies in an upstairs bunker, its further distribution, including the ascent to the tower, rested with the housemaids. The under-housemaid was further responsible for the schoolroom breakfast, in the days when the schoolroom functioned. Flora MacTavish, in the laundry, was out of the public eye, but her standards may be judged by the fact that she would spend a full hour making up a single dress-shirt. The chief heroine, however, was the kitchen-maid – she had to be up at six, to light the kitchen fire to heat the morning bathwater, as well, no doubt, as to prepare early tea for her seniors; and her work would probably never have been finished at all if my mother had not ruled that young people needed adequate sleep, and that she must be free to go to bed by ten o'clock. It was, in fact, on this account that we had dinner at half-past seven, even in the long light evenings of the northern summer, in order to allow washing-up to be achieved at a reasonable hour.

The day began with the ringing, at half-past eight, of a very large bell, which hung in a slate-roofed housing outside the pantry and was tolled from inside by the tablemaid by means of a rope and pulley. Strangely enough, inside this part of the house one heard the creaking of the pulley more loudly than the bell itself. The servants' breakfast had been signalled at eight o'clock with a sharper-toned brass handbell. The big bell went again at quarter-past nine, this time for prayers, which my father read and which took about five minutes; breakfast must have been already sizzling in the background, as it appeared immediately afterwards although the upper servants had attended prayers. The only point about breakfast that deserves record is that we ate our porridge out of bowls, not

plates, and while walking about the dining-room; this practice
surprised English guests, though it was, I believe, perfectly
normal in the Highlands, and it was no odder than the Swedish
custom of eating hors d'oeuvres at a sideboard. (In Sweden
I once ate no less than three successive courses standing up
at a side-table – hors d'oeuvres, spinach and omelette, with
schnapps and beer and a song sung to the schnapps – before
sitting down to the soup, with which there was port.) Our
eggs were cooked by steam in a globe-shaped silver boiler,
the hardness or softness of the eggs ideally depending on the
quantity of methylated spirit measured into the burner.

What happened in the course of the morning depended a
good deal on the season of the year, the weather, and the
number and types of people who were staying in the house.
Some of us might still have been pursuing some form of
education, some of the rest were energetic, keen for long
walks on the hill, and others elderly or badly in need of rest.
In August and earlier September the grouse were, of course,
a matter of prime importance, while at Christmas there were
pheasants, woodcock and rough shooting in general. Fearfully
wet weather in the summer brought a bonus in the shape of
spates and fishing in the burn. In reasonable weather the
least energetic could sit in chairs in the garden, my mother
having these arrangements very well organised according to
the direction of the wind and the position of the sun; even a tent
was available for use when the sun was too strong for reading
without protection. My mother herself was endlessly busy
with household and village affairs, some of which naturally
devolved on available members of the family; the flowers
for the house, for example, were picked and arranged by
daughters, though the tablemaids had the job of clearing up
the pantry afterwards, and of washing the bowls and vases.
Pot plants were raised in the greenhouse, and brought in by
one of the gardeners. When nothing offered in the way of
outdoor activity, the company tended to sort itself out more
or less by age and sex; older women settled in my mother's
morning-room, older men and uncles found their way to the

library, while the younger generation disposed itself largely in the billiard-room, or in the schoolroom when this was no longer in use as such. The drawing-room was not ordinarily used until after lunch, its fire not being lighted until half-past twelve instead of first thing in the morning, as were those of the other public rooms.

On Sundays the routine was different, as no family prayers were said and a more formal service was held at eleven o'clock. For this the hall was cleared, chairs were set out in rows, and not only the servants attended but also gardeners and others in from outside. My father read Morning Prayer from the Episcopal prayer-book, tactfully substituting 'ministers of Thy Word' for 'bishops, priests and deacons' to meet Presbyterian scruples. The persistence of childhood impressions is shown by the fact that I still feel 'bishops, priests and deacons' to be somehow anomalous. We sang two hymns, for which my mother played a harmonium with treadle bellows, and nobody attempted a sermon.

By my time, the traditional Sabbath had lost many of its sharpest teeth; hardly anyone in the village now sat behind drawn blinds on Sunday afternoons, and many people went out for sedate walks or visited their family graves. The day was past when a perfectionist like my father's old nurse would allow a little boy to do nothing on Sunday but draw pictures of churches and ministers. None the less, local feelings about Sunday observance still had to be reckoned with. Shooting or fishing was, of course, unthinkable, and boats were not taken out – this last reasonably enough, as pulling a boat down the beach would have meant work for a gardener. Bicycles were a borderline case, and I never remember riding a bicycle on Sunday. The women of the family sometimes registered embarrassment about knitting and sewing, at least in front of the servants, and we used to put the cards and card-table away at bedtime on Saturday nights to save the housemaids from contact with them when they tidied things up the next morning.

Sunday morning, in fine weather, was often made an

occasion for taking the time by the sun. In those days, it was sometimes difficult to be sure of Greenwich time, and my father accordingly made use of a sun-sextant, an instrument in which two images of the sun, reflected in a pair of mirrors, converged when the sun was at its zenith. This took place at Skipness approximately twenty-one minutes and twenty-one seconds later than it did at Greenwich, and this allowance plus some further corrections taken from a table yielded the desired result. This instrument was later superseded by a simpler and less scientific one, which could be used at any time of day and not only at noon; it worked by directing a spot of light, through a hole in a movable fitment, on to a scale graded plainly in hours and minutes, so that no calculations were needed.

Lunch came at half-past one, again announced by the bell. The lunch of those days differed from a modern lunch mainly in the fact that nobody thought of drinking anything beforehand. Sherry was known in our house purely as a wine drunk at dinner with the fish; a maid brought it round immediately after the fish-dish as today she might bring hock. If cocktails had yet crossed the Atlantic, they had not reached the tribal areas. In fact I drank my first cocktail only in 1910, in no more probable a place than the Kaiserlicher Automobilklub in Berlin. Otherwise lunch was a substantial meal with, probably, a choice of hot meats if the party was a big one, and cold ham or grouse on the sideboard, and then sweets and cheese. Claret and whisky and soda were the ordinary drinks, apart from water; a barrel of beer for the servants had existed in the cellar in my childhood, but I remember neither draught nor bottled beer in the dining-room, and cider and the gassy drinks had probably not come into fashion. Whisky, of course, was drunk much more commonly than today, and in fact the period was only recently past when a tot of whisky had ranked, in Highland etiquette, as a kind of honourable gratuity to casual outdoor men. As demand fell off, the cask was replaced by bottles, but the whisky was always handed in a heavy cut-glass decanter.

After lunch most of the women, at any rate, would probably

The sea-route to Skipness, 1877.
below Morning sun on the Old House, winter 1877.

The Castle before 1892. Sketch by John Bannerman, coachman, whose quarters were inside the courtyard up to 1883. *below* The Castle and House of 1881, photographed in 1899, after excavation and restoration by R.C. Graham. (National Monuments Record of Scotland)

The Hall, 1881. On the
settee, the photographer-
laird R.C. Graham.
below The Good Life,
1887. R.C. Graham's
paraphernalia as artist,
author, fencer, book and
picture collector; also his
walking stick, his gun and
a deerskin.

Angus Graham aged about four, with Father's stick, in conventional
pose on Avenue bridge over the Small Burn *c.*1896.

clockwise from below
Skipness musicians:
Frances Graham piping
for dancers Phyllis Rose
and Joey Lang; Punch and
Judy with banjos; Frances
Graham, chanter; Ethel
Graham, piccolo, 1900;
and the House of 1881,
photographed in 1900.
The suspended dummy is a
typical Skipness jape.

Angus Graham aged about ten.

Loading sheep at the Pier, 1905. In the background Bannerman has brought his Master and Mistress to watch from below the Pier House.

Unloading cargo, perhaps coal, on the shore below the House.
Fishing boats, some at anchor, lie offshore.
below Sheep going to wintering from the Pier, autumn 1906.

Spearing flounders, 1905. R.F. Graham rowing, Frances Graham with three-pronged leister in her right hand. *below, from left* Standing: R.C. Graham, Gerard Collier, unknown. Seated: Frances Graham, 'Uncle Bob' (Robert Collier), Lord Monkswell, Angus Graham, Emily E. Graham, Ethel Graham (with Mumsy Bess and puppies), Lady Mary Monkswell (diarist).

Sunday afternoon, September 1905. Angus Graham, in sun-hat beside his Mother with parasol. R.C. Graham far right.

Tug-of-war, Claonaig Sports, 1905.
On left, R.F. Graham; on right, Angus Graham.

At the Flower Show, 1906. From left, Bertram Vaughan Johnson,
Angus Graham and Owen O'Malley (first cousin).

Gertrude Vaughan Johnson, in perambulator, at the Flower Show, 1907.

Outdoor knitting in the garden, August 1907. Emily Graham with rugs *and* parasol.

Kilbrannan Chapel, 1907. From left: Ethel Graham, knitting as usual, Frances Graham, Angus Graham, R.C. Graham.

R.F. Graham and Angus Graham, then a Staff Officer,
Highland Light Infantry, 1915.

After the War. R.F. Graham fishing, Claonaig Bum, 1920.

The Village in 1920. Note sea-pool, former joint mouth of Skibble
and Crow Glen Burns, also outdoor knitting still in progress.

Haymakers pose for photographer beside post office on Caolfin road, 1920. below Carters resting beside the High Road near Glenbuie.

Pier House, Pier and Minard Castle, 1920.

Cautious embarkation of passengers at the Pier, 1920.

move to the drawing-room, to drink coffee in the bow-window and look at the view. This window was one of the best things in the house, as it held six or eight people sitting on curved upholstered seats which fitted the shape of the turret, and commanded not only the garden but the whole east side of Kintyre to beyond Campbeltown, the Sound of Kilbrannan, the Arran mountains, the Castle, the Chapel and the Point. Further off, beyond the Sound of Bute, were the Garroch Head and the dim Ayrshire coastline. On a round table in the centre of the turret there stood a very large brass telescope, which showed every detail of craft entering or passing the Bay – fishing boats anchored until sunset, sometimes a pair of boats fishing illegally by daylight, 'herring-buyer' steamers lying to, and sometimes a yacht sending people ashore to call or to visit the Castle. In the course of the afternoon my mother usually went for a walk, or a drive in the carriage, the latter particularly if she had some call to make at the southern end of the estate.

Unless a tea-picnic was decreed (p.101), tea was a sit-down meal with toast, scones, jam, honey, cake and so on. It took place at five o'clock, either in the schoolroom or the hall, according to the size of the party. A really large party, perhaps with callers from outside, might demand two teapots and an enormous silver urn, fired by methylated spirit. With tea was apt to coincide the arrival of the post, heralded by the hearty tones of Sandy Thomson the postman conversing with the maids through one of the courtyard windows. Our postal arrangements deserve a word of record as a fine Victorian survival. The letters came by sea to Tarbert, were carried thence to Whitehouse by the three-horse Campbeltown coach, and were picked up there by our postman about one o'clock, or later if the steamer was late. His pony-cart might reach Skipness, with luck, by four o'clock, and the letters reached the House about an hour later. As Sandy lived at the Pier, he must often have got home very late, particularly on stormy winter evenings. His start was correspondingly early, as he had to deliver the outgoing mail at Whitehouse before the northgoing coach passed at about eleven. This coach was superseded in 1913; I remember reading in the *Continental Daily Mail*, somewhere in Austria, that 'the last stage-coach in Britain' had gone off the road, though I cannot vouch for the truth of its having been really the last.

After tea the energetic often played tennis, or in winter one had time for conversation in front of the fire. People with letters requiring immediate answer had to get to work on them at once, as 'Sandy Post' called at half-past eight in the morning. There were also the papers to be read, as in default of wireless we had heard no news through the day. Our papers were *The Times* and *The Glasgow Herald*, with two local weeklies, *The Campbeltown Courier* and the 'Squeak', properly *The Argyllshire Advertiser and Lochfyneside Echo*. Nobody thought of sherry, or any other drinks before dinner. The bell rang for dressing at seven o'clock, and in the bedrooms dress-clothes were laid out ready on the beds, with cans of hot water keeping warm in cosies on the wash-stands. There was never any question of not dressing for dinner.

The distance from the drawing-room to the dining-room – along the gallery and down the long front stair – was considered too great to be navigated arm-in-arm, so the allotment of partners was postponed until the company had reached the hall. It assembled first in the drawing-room, when the dinner-bell rang, and moved downstairs when the table-maid opened the door and announced 'Dinner is ready'; my mother made a point of her not saying 'Dinner is served', which she rightly considered vulgar, pointing out its difference from the phrase *'Madame est servie'*. The meal was again substantial; in fact the amount that people ate in the ordinary way now seems surprisingly large. A menu, written by my mother on a china 'slate', stood at each end of the table and was passed round for inspection, and for anyone to miss out a course was perfectly normal. For a large party there might well have been six courses and dessert – for example, soup, fish or entrée but probably not both, meat, grouse or some other game at suitable seasons, and sweet or savoury. Failing game, there might have been both sweet and savoury. Mutton, vegetables and fruit were all raised on the estate, but other meat came from the electrician-butcher. Fish might be difficult, unless we caught it ourselves, as the herring fishermen ordinarily sold their catch onto buyers' boats at sea. When they did bring any of it ashore, herrings cost a penny each. Drinks were very much as at lunch, probably claret or hock with whisky and soda to fall back upon, and port or marsala with dessert; nobody seemed to think twice about drinking port and whisky. The men were generally in the drawing-room by a quarter to nine, and the rest of the evening was devoted to conversation, cards, round games, or some kind of music. Bridge was just coming in. Nobody faded away to get on with work or correspondence, whatever they may have had to sit down to when they reached their bedrooms. Whisky and a siphon appeared about half-past ten, formal good-nights were said, and everyone collected a candle with a saucer candlestick to light the way to his room.

Note: The illustration at the opening of the chapter shows the author's mother, and her mother-in-law, and is taken from a drawing by his father.

12. THE GARDENS AND POLICIES

The history of the front garden seems to be completely lost. The existence of a garden as early as 1727 is proved, as has been said, by the gardener's headstone in the graveyard; and in view of this Langlands' omission of a garden-enclosure from his map of 1801 may be attributed either to error or to the smallness of the map's scale. In 1833 William Dobie noted a garden in front of the house which produced flowers, fruit and vegetables; and this record, combined with his sketch, notwithstanding the latter's topographical inaccuracy, suggests that the area was sheltered from the worst of the sea-winds by a protective plantation of trees. Apart from these hints we have no evidence earlier than the OS map of 1867, and any features shown on it may naturally derive either from the later Campbells or from the Frasers. It seems most likely on the whole that large-scale construction or reconstruction in the garden would have been done by whoever enlarged the original Old House, and it has been suggested above that this, in turn, may have been the work of the seventh or eighth Campbell laird, in the middle of the eighteenth century. However that may be, the shape of the garden has not changed since 1867 and the protective trees on the south and south-west still stand, while sixty years ago the internal arrangements, too, corresponded with the older pattern more closely than they do today. It should also be noted here that the stretch of the small burn just outside the garden wall has been confined to an artificial course, and that this conforms to the wall's own line in a way which suggests that both result from a common plan. This was the state of affairs in 1867, and at that time the burn's lowermost stretch formed a small lagoon between the south wall of the garden and the storm-beach; at some time later than 1867, however, a direct outlet for the burn was cut through the storm-beach and the lagoon was gradually filled up with ash-pit debris from the House. Today the burn has returned to something like its earlier line, the storm-beach having re-formed and obliterated the artificial outlet of which no trace survives. The canalisation of the burn where it passes the garden must have saved the field to the west from periodical flooding, if not also the ground on the east that is now inside the garden, as pools of water still appear in the field on rare occasions, when a heavy spate coincides with a very high tide and an onshore gale. In fact, it seems possible that before the burn was controlled something in the nature of a permanent marsh may have existed behind this part of the storm-beach, in the manner of the Snipe Pond of the east side of the garden, even perhaps extending right across to the larger burn. Such conditions would naturally have had an important effect on the siting of any early settlement.

The garden lay at two levels, directly by an artificial grass bank five hundred and ninety feet long and about seven feet high, aligned approximately from west-north-west to east-south-east;* this was evidently laid out parallel to the frontage of the Old House, which had stood close to its lip, and it is likewise parallel to that of the New House, which kept to the same alignment, though standing about a hundred and seventeen feet further back. The intervening space, on which the Old House stood, is occupied by lawns and gravel paths. The bank is steep, and a flight of red-sandstone steps mounts it at the point that was immediately in front of the entrance to the Old House, and not in the middle of the garden, though the gravel path that continues from the bottom of the steps, at right angles to the bank, has been treated as the garden's north-south axis. The east-west axis is formed by a second gravel path, which crosses the first at right angles about a

---

* Treated below as east and west for convenience.

hundred and thirty feet below the steps; and a third path runs
along the inside of the south wall, from the south-west corner
to a point near the south-east corner where it joins the east-west
axis. The area, which measures about two hundred and forty by
six hundred and fifty feet along the axis-paths, thus consists of
four divisions very unequal in size. The north-west one, nearly
rectangular, contained, on the west, a plantation of big hardwood
trees, largely sycamore, and between this and the central path a
formal rose-garden with a fountain in the middle. The south-west
division, an irregular five-sided figure larger than the first, held
further protective hardwood, and an orchard of apples and pears.
The north-eastern division contained a formal arrangement of
flowerbeds, and at its east end a stretch of grass large enough
to hold a tennis court; until about 1890 a greenhouse had stood
here, but it was then moved to the west end of the garden
frontage of the House. A still earlier greenhouse was represented
by a potting-shed just inside the south-east gate to the shore, the
remains of a tank in the floor testifying to its former function. The
south-east division was a small triangle of grass, planted with a
few shrubs.

The existence of the garden depended on shelter from the
wind, and this was provided by the wall, about ten feet high;
by the thin belt of small sycamores that ran along the wall's
inner side, and had had their heads cut back by the wind
as soon as they looked over its top; and by the large trees
west of the fountain and orchard. Easterly winds were further
checked by a double line of shrubbery with trees, including
overgrown beech hedges, which flanked both sides of the
central walk, forming a north-south windbreak about fifty
feet wide. Among other things, a clump of bamboo and a
camellia flourished in this shrubbery for years, showing, like
the myrtle bush outside the morning-room window, how mild
the West Highland climate really was. Between the shrubbery
and the high trees to the west lay the four beds of the rose
garden, bordered outside with the fuchsia which grows so
commonly in the West; their outer corners were squared,
and their inner sides curved to the circumference of a circle

centred on the fountain. The rose garden was greatly favoured as a place to put garden chairs, for sitting out in fine weather. The fountain, which was installed shortly before 1890, had in the middle a cement figure of a boy riding on a tortoise; it leaked incurably, muddying the turf round about, and was finally left dry. By that time the tame wild-duck had, I think, already been disestablished, as they reduced the fountain to the condition of a farmyard puddle. The ground under the trees, beyond the rose garden, was kept more or less wild, though the grass was scythed periodically and spring bulbs were set out in it in clumps – snowdrops, daffodils, bluebells, crocuses and dogtooth violets. The formal garden east of the central walk was used for bedding out; its corners were defined by large beds backed by escallonia and fuchsia, and inside these was an arrangement of smaller ones, of various geometrical shapes. The bedded-out plants were a standing temptation to young rabbits, still small enough to squeeze through wire netting, and, more particularly, to roe deer, which made nothing of jumping the fences of the upper lawn until these were strengthened and raised. But the chief feature of this part of the garden was a great, spreading monkey-puzzle. In the middle or earlier years of the nineteenth century *Araucaria imbricata* was fashionable, and whoever laid out these beds, presumably my grandmother, evidently meant to have a monkey-puzzle growing at each end of the system, like the masts of a ship. However, the tree at the east end died, while its congener, sheltered by the neighbouring central shrubbery, grew to unexampled proportions, and eventually began to incur an increasing volume of criticism. It was generally admitted to be ugly, sinister, far too big, and quite out of keeping with its setting, but it had managed to impose its personality on everyone so firmly that sentence was never pronounced. When my brother sold the estate in 1936, he said to the new owner, 'Cut down the monkey-puzzle now; if you delay, it will get you'.

The red-sandstone steps were built of old, weathered blocks, no doubt taken from the Castle. They thus provided plenty of crannies and cavities, in which were established small clumps of delicate Trichomenes fern.

The apple-house at the south-west corner of the garden has somehow acquired a bogus piece of folklore, as it was said to have been, in origin, a joiner's workshop, and sounds suggestive of the nailing-up of coffins were believed to come from it at night. This story falls down of itself as the building is shown by the OS maps to date from later than 1867, and any early carpenter's shop, whether the source of the coffin-making noises or not, was probably in one of the houses near the mill. This is, in fact, where Mrs Higginson puts it in her version of the story. It is true that an unexplained noise was sometimes heard by people, myself included, who slept in rooms facing the garden; but this noise resembled the clink of a chisel on stone, and was quite different from the duller sound of nails being driven into wood.

The kitchen-garden was made by my grandmother, soon after she came to Skipness. It stands on a gentle south-facing slope, about a quarter of a mile from the House, is almost square in shape and extends to just over an acre within a high stone wall. Outside the west wall there is an annexe contained by a hedge, and another hedged strip on the south. The ground inside the wall was divided into four by paths on the two main axes, while other paths ran parallel with the walls and subdivided the four main blocks. All the paths were gravelled, and were edged with dwarf box. The central north-south path, flanked by beds containing herbaceous plants, led from a door in the south wall to the east end of a greenhouse built against the west half of the north wall; at the top of this path, by the greenhouse door, there was a rock-garden for Alpine plants. The garden as a whole was mainly devoted to vegetables, and fruit in season; raspberries, in particular, assumed the proportions of a forest along the south side and presented an enormous problem in netting against blackbirds and thrushes. The strawberry beds were in one of the upper blocks, and were likewise closely netted; much time was spent in disentangling birds from the netting without damage to their fragile anatomies. Gooseberries and currants, too, gave quite heavy crops. Fruit-trees, mainly apples, with some plums, greengages and cherries, were trained on the walls, and some standard apple-trees stood in the beds in the middle of the garden. The greenhouse was divided into three, the hottest part being on the west where it adjoined the furnace in a potting-shed outside the garden-wall. The three parts contained, in order from hot to cooler, first melons and cucumbers, each melon supported individually on a small square of slate, then grapes and tomatoes, and finally peaches and nectarines. All were excellent while their rather short seasons lasted.

The annexe outside the west wall contained both flowers and vegetables, with cold frames, a manure-heap and, at the top, a row of beehives, including some old straw skeps, in a long roofed shelter. This had earlier stood near the centre of the walled garden. Asparagus did remarkably well, as the large bed of it was always manured with seaweed. The annexe was notable for a splendid hedge of clipped yew, which ran for some two hundred and sixty feet parallel to the garden wall and about thirty feet from it, with a path and flanking beds lying between them. It measured about eight feet in height by five feet in thickness, and was densely grown and cut square at the top; while in the middle two squared 'towers' rose four or five feet higher, flanking a transverse path.

The head gardener was named John Turner, and something must be said about him and his colleagues in the gardens. Turner was not a Highlander, having been brought in from outside by my grandmother – I think, from Greenock. I remember him as a shortish, stocky man with a red beard turning grey; extremely friendly and kind, and full of genial talk. He had a habit of alluding to himself in the third person, and signed letters with his surname only, like a peer. He took great pride in his vegetables, and hated spoiling the show that they made in the garden by bringing them in for use; peas in particular, he begrudged deeply to the dining-room before they had reached full size and total solidity. Turner's great quality was his skill at extraneous jobs, quite unconnected with gardening; in fact he was always happiest when doing something other than his normal work, for example, rowing the boat, making the acetylene gas, or stoking the hot-pipe furnace. Somehow he succeeded better at outside jobs than he did in the niceties of gardening, some of which bored him; my mother had been known, on failing to find him anywhere, to feel the seat of his potting-shed chair to find out whether it was warm, showing that he had just vacated it and fled into hiding when he saw her coming up the path. He once said to her bitterly, 'Turner has been working wi' weemin for forty years, and he's never pleased them yet'.

Of lesser men in the gardens, one recalls the MacCallum family, fishermen who had given up the sea with the decline of the herring fishery. Old Archie MacCallum's career must have started in the days of the Campbells, and his sons, John, Sandy and Archie, all worked in the garden at one time or another. Archie, the youngest, persisted until fairly recent times. Owing to a plethora of MacCallums, these sons were always identified by their father's Christian name, as for example, 'Archie Archie' and not as 'Archie MacCallum'. This practice was in fact quite common, and sometimes a mother's name could be used in place of a father's, as in the case of 'Sandy Jean', but such a form as 'Teenie Sanitary', for the daughter of a sanitary inspector,* must have been exceptional. Another ex-fisherman, Allan MacMillan, also doubled as a gardener from time to time, though functioning as well as handyman about the House, where he occupied himself with boots, coal and firewood, and the trundling of debris in a barrow out to the ash-heap.

South of the garden lay the rest of the policies proper, an area of open-growing hardwoods through which ran the avenue. The trees were probably planted and the avenue organised in its present form by the elder Fraser laird, though Mrs

---

* This name appears in a work of fiction (Bridge, A., *And Then You Came*, 1942) but is vouched for as authentic by the authoress.

Robert Campbell states that the avenue was being improved in 1813; Fraser, at any rate, is credited with having installed the gate-posts at the entrance to the avenue, a most unhappy product of the fashion for misusing cast iron. The supposed gatekeeper's lodge, in which Turner and his wife lived for many years, is a further monument to the taste of the same period, being a kind of sub-Norman pillbox which apes the Castle's grey rubble walls and red-sandstone dressings. The avenue obliterates the lade that carried water to the mill (p.53), and this suggests that milling came to an end in the 1840s.

Overlooking the avenue from rising ground a short distance west of the garden were the stables and coachman's house. The stables for the carriage-horses were the first buildings that my father cleared out of the Castle courtyard, of which they had previously occupied the north-west corner; the date of their removal was about 1883 or 1884. The new stables, now a garage, comprised a main block, with coach-houses below and a flat for the coachman above, and a wing, abutting its west gable, which contained stalls for three horses, a loose-box, a harness-room and a loft for fodder. An open-ended shed of corrugated iron was added many years later, for the washing of carriages in bad weather. We kept two horses, and the choice of vehicles lay between a waggonette, convertible into a bus by the fitting of a massive top; a victoria with a tarpaulin hood, which could take luggage on the box and on the backwards-facing seat; and a two-wheeled dog-cart. The bus, fully loaded, was as much as a pair could manage, and its customary time for the journey to Tarbert pier, of thirteen miles and a half, was well over two hours; the victoria might take under two hours, and the dog-cart a good deal less. The drive to Tarbert could be a most wearisome business, especially on stormy days when one suffered either the horsy fug of the bus or rain or snow on the box. The coachman, Thomas Bannerman, conducted this circus faultlessly for something like forty years, and never had an accident of any description on the road. He grew a fine *gloire-de-Dijon* rose up the front of his house, and kept a white cockatoo, which was set outside in its cage on sunny days and made conversation to visitors.

The horses were disestablished in 1913, and their place was taken by a Belsize car of magnificent weight and solidity. It could take three different forms – a two seater, when the back was vacant; an estate-car, with a home-made wooden box-back; and a four-seater when a high back-seat was fitted in place of the box. The whole could be closed in with a heavy canvas hood, and when all these fittings were in place, and with four passengers and luggage, one sometimes felt less than confident about getting up some of the hills. Splendidly built as it was, in massive steel and brass, the engine suffered from the drawback of requiring two people to start it, one to crank the starting-handle round and round – and smartly too, as the ignition was by magneto – while the other sat at the controls to manipulate throttle and spark. It was also essential to block a certain air-intake with a bundle of rags, attached to a piece of string, and this the man at the handle had to snatch away when the crucial moment arrived. The gears were of a modern pattern, though the notch for 'reverse' had to be opened by pulling up a brass ring; the lamps burned acetylene gas, and the horn really was a horn, of brass with a rubber bulb.

Notwithstanding the bundle of rags and pneumatic horn, this old Belsize was modern compared with the Arrol-Johnston dog-cart, owned by Cousin William Crum, with which we had become acquainted a few years earlier. This wonderful machine was still in the horse-drawn tradition, and seemed to accept its engine only under protest. Of substantial wooden construction, it had high dog-cart wheels with projecting iron hub-caps and solid rubber tyres; dashboards, armrests and so on were all of coachbuilder's patterns; and below the front seat there was a long, up-tilted footboard, as if to protect the passengers from mud kicked backwards by a horse. Two passengers sat here, facing forwards without a windscreen; behind them was the driver, with another passenger beside him, and on the back seat two more, facing backwards. The engine was under the driver, and was started by pulling up a rope through a hole in the floor. Of the car's real capacities nothing was known, as Cousin William, a law-abiding man, had had a governor fitted which kept speed down automatically to twelve miles an hour, at that time the legal limit.

Two men are unfailingly connected with my memories of our first car, Neil Maclachlan and his brother Duncan. Neil was a sawmill mechanic whom my brother engaged as chauffeur and taught to drive; in later years he rose to the position of factor and married Jean Wilson, my mother's maid and one of the family descended from the old Campbell laird's daughter (p.62). Duncan had once been a blacksmith but was now practically an invalid; he had married another of my mother's maids, Jean Scott, who had charge of the post office, and he stepped into the breach when Neil went into the army. He had all the West Highlander's capacity for making things go on a shoestring, and when some part of the car appeared to need repair or replacement, would protest that 'it might stand a long time'.

Before the days of motoring we depended a good deal on bicycles, but of these only one deserves record, my father's so-called 'Bantam'. The Bantam marked an early step in evolution away from the high 'penny-farthing' and towards the modern bicycle; and it showed its ancestry in the absence of sprocket-wheel and chain, and in the setting of the pedals on the axle of the front wheel. The revolutions of pedals and wheel were somehow adjusted to a supposedly suitable ratio by a gear inside the axle. The wheels were smallish and the saddle was consequently low, and this combined with the forward position of the pedals greatly reduced the thrust exerted by the rider; but a more serious fault resided in the fore-and-aft trim, as a result of which the back wheel was constantly liable to kick up, throwing the rider forwards on to his head. No-one ever tried the Bantam more than once.

Note: The drawing at the opening of the chapter shows Thomas Bannerman, the coachman, on the New Road, and is taken from a photograph after 1885. Bannerman made the sketch of the Castle which appears as plate 3.

13. THE SHORE AND THE POINT

If the first step out of the House was into the garden, a second and very short one led on to the shore. The shore was immensely convenient, and the change of scene was total. One had simply to open the door in the wall at the south-east corner of the garden, or raise the latch and have the door blown in by the wind, to find oneself standing on the crown of the beach with the whole of the Sound before one, and Arran beyond. Even the grass was different from garden grass, being a fine seaside turf; sea-campion grew along the beach-head, and sea buckthorn in the Chapel graveyard in the field behind. The works of man were limited to the garden-wall and the boat-house, with perhaps a boat pulled up above high-water mark, and an enormous anchor whose purpose I never discovered. The beach was of rolled gravel, white and grey, and was contoured with lines of dead seaweed and wave-borne rubbish – a lower belt at ordinary high-water level, and an upper one left by storms. The gravel sloped down gently, coarser above and finer and sandier below, to give place at the bottom to a flat expanse of sand marked with sandworm casts, which might run out for fifty yards or more at the lowest of the springs.

I think of this stretch of foreshore largely in terms of its birds. The commonest were probably the ringed plovers and oystercatchers, one or two pairs of both of which nested on it regularly; and over the course of the year one might see curlews, redshanks, common and purple sandpipers, turnstones and dunlins, with green and golden plovers paying occasional visits from the fields inland. The dead seaweed also attracted some land-birds, such as rock pipits and starlings, no doubt on account of the hoppers, unpleasant creatures like large fleas, that lived underneath it. Gulls were always on the spot – common, herring, black-headed and lesser black-backed – but greater blackbacks appeared only now and then, and were so cautious that they generally kept to the middle distance. The ringed plovers were protectively coloured, and consequently difficult to spot on the gravel beach; their speckled eggs, like those of the oyster-catchers, matched the shingle exactly, and the best way to find their nests, bare hollows trimmed with a few pieces of seaweed, was to detect the old bird stealing surreptitiously away. I possess a photograph of two newly-hatched oyster-catcher chicks, taken long ago by my father, which shows how they tone into their background; their legs are disproportionately long from birth, like a foal's legs, to allow them to run at the earliest possible moment. If one came too close to a ringed plover's nest or young, the old bird would sometimes put on the familiar act with an apparently broken wing.

The Point consists of two ridges of rock, both running seawards and separated by the large inlet of Sandy Bay. Low tide uncovers a great stretch of sand here, with a single big rounded boulder, no doubt dropped by a glacier. The first ridge closes the end of Skipness Bay proper; the second, on the east side of Sandy Bay, is longer and wider than the first, and east of it again there lie two tidal islets, whalebacks of rock more or less parallel with the ridges. The inner one of these, which is never fully submerged, can be reached at every low tide across a narrow strip of sand; the outer one dries out only at the bottom of springs, and then gives a strange impression of really belonging to the sea, and only showing itself in the upper air by some kind of enchantment. The rocks were thickly sown with small tidal pools, containing every kind of lovely marine growth, all on a miniature scale, with dark-red sea-anemones and small bushes of weed which sheltered numbers of prawns. Prawns make an entrancing quarry for a small boy, as they are masters of evasion by means of sudden backwards jerks; they are also much nicer for tea than winkles, of which there were millions to be had, once the technique of extracting the winkle with a pin has lost its novelty. Occasionally a pool might hold a very small fish, probably with a bulldog head and big frilly fins like wings.

The coast, as has been said, turns from east to north on the far side of the rocks, and the next inlet, Shell Bay, is quite different from Sandy Bay though only about a hundred yards from it. The flat tidal sands are replaced by stones and rock-outcrops, all supporting a good deal of slippery weed; the beach, just above and below high-water mark, is largely composed of shells broken up fine, with many small and delicate ones still perfectly intact. Small cowries sometimes turn up, as they do also, for that matter, though less frequently, in Sandy Bay. Between Shell and Sandy Bays there is a single high sand-dune, grassed over except on its south-west side; here there is a steep face of bare sand, probably dug away long ago to form a rabbit-warren. The neighbouring hinterland, an area of seaside turf, rock-outcrops and marshy depressions heavily grown with bog-myrtle, generally supported at least one nest of shelduck, and probably of mallard and merganser; mergansers are very poor mothers, and one used to watch the young family decreasing in size day by day as the casualties mounted. Herons sometimes inspected the rock-pools and tidal shallows, and offshore there might be gannets, cormorants, shags, guillemots and red-throated divers. Seals occasionally landed to lie on the rocks, but more often only showed a cautious head at a safe distance from the shore. Basking sharks were not uncommon, their tall back-fins often sailing past quite close inshore, but I believe that they were harmless to anything larger than a herring; porpoises sometimes got entangled in the fishermen's nets, or gambolled too close to rowing-boats for their occupants' peace of mind.

I have said that for fish we depended largely on ourselves, and this was one of the extra-horticultural duties that Turner performed so well. He and Old Archie MacCallum managed the boats, and all that we knew of sea-fishing we learned from them. One could either row the boat about over a selected beat, trolling a white lure behind, or else one could anchor and fish on the bottom bait. The former method eliminated the need for bait, and sometimes attracted mackerel, but the latter produced a greater weight of possibly inferior fish – coal-fish and pollack, which we called saithe and lythe. A very small cod occasionally blundered in, or a plaice if we happened to have anchored over the sand, but the most favoured spot was off the end of the western ridge of the Point, where the bottom was rocky and weed-grown. The tackle consisted of two hooks, baited with mussels, hanging from the ends of a disused umbrella-rib, set horizontally on the end of the line, and with a weight between them on a slightly longer attachment; this contraption was lowered until the weight touched the bottom and was then drawn up two feet, the baits being thus supposedly brought up to the height from the bottom most likely to interest the fish. I was electrified to find the Indians using this very same method when fishing for salmon in salt water off the coast of Vancouver Island. A much more interesting fishery was the spearing of flounders and plaice (see plate 16), which could only be done when the sea was glassily calm and the fish could be seen on the bottom as the boat drifted over. The best ground was the sand in the Bay just below low-water mark, and was limited by the depth that could be reached with a twelve-foot spear; the flounders lay with the greater part of their bodies lightly covered with sand, and what one saw was consequently no more than a ghostly outline with a nose and two eyes at one end. For a successful stroke with the three-pronged spear the approach had to be extremely stealthy, as the fish were very much alert, and would whisk away in a moment. Very small flounders, of half-crown size but already thoroughly flattened and with both their eyes trained upwards, sometimes appeared in the sandy sea-pools of the Skipness and Claonaig Burns.

It is impossible to end this chapter without adding a word about the quantity and quality of the things that got washed up on the shore. Skipness possessing no shops apart from the post office and one small 'general merchant', it was often impossible to make minor deficiencies good without writing to Glasgow or London. One consequently fell into the habit of botching up replacements with such materials as came conveniently to hand, and for this purpose a walk along the line of the high-water jetsam was frequently well worth while. Sailors must have lost or thrown away an astonishing range of objects in wood, rubber and metal, to say nothing of furniture and clothing. 'Where did you get that?' someone might ask, in admiration of a useful possession, and the answer would come, 'I picked it up on the shore'. Colonel James Craig, later Lord Craigavon, used to take the shooting at Claonaig, and one summer he gave a fancy-dress dinner to which my brother and sister went disguised as tramps. They dressed entirely in clothes which they had found on the shore, and had subsequently dowsed with peat-smoke; they knocked at the back door instead of approaching the front, and took everyone in completely. The dogs hardly got over it.

14. THE GLENS AND WOODS

Whatever may be thought of the Romantic approach in general, there is no denying the benefit that it brought to Skipness in promoting the organisation of the glens and outer policies. Someone – it is not known who, or exactly when, or whether in one go or over a period of years – but someone who was clearly a Romantic planted ornamental woods, laid out paths for the use of ladies and children on dignified family walks, and built bridges and steps and at least one fine gazebo.

The nearest glen to the House to receive this treatment was the one formed by the burn that runs down past the Castle. The path left the avenue at the bridge just below the Castle, and ran up the right bank of the burn past a cottage which exemplified the old plan of dwelling and byre in line under the same roof. Here, rather than in the village, was perhaps the relic of a 'castleton', through which, in the days before the village took shape along the road from Claonaig, the track from Glenreasdell may have approached the Castle. The last inhabitants of this cottage were a ploughman, John Campbell, and his considerably older wife; they occupied a large place in the scheme of my childhood as John was a very kind friend, who made me bows and arrows which really worked, while Mrs Campbell told pungent stories even after she was bedridden with a broken hip. The right bank was level and easy in this lower part of the glen, the left being steep and broken by cliffs of red clay; higher up the conditions were reversed, with the cliffs on the right, now higher and more continuous, and to avoid them the path crossed the burn by

97

a solid stone bridge. Opposite the highest of the cliffs there was a wooden 'summer-house' with a thatched roof and a seat inside, and nearby a circular seat arranged round the base of a big beech-tree. The path eventually led out on to the Pier Road, after passing a small pond once used for the retting of flax, of which a good deal seems to have been grown in Argyll at the beginning of the nineteenth century. The wood in the glen was mixed beech and sycamore, and some of the largest trees were probably planted as early as about 1800, though the bulk of the stand may have been rather younger.

The hollow of the glen flattened out above the Pier Road, the upper reaches of the burn being shallow and rocky. Immediately above the road it traversed a plantation of confiners, formed since 1867, and inside this was the reservoir that supplied piped water to the House and farm. To insure against the burn running dry in an exceptional drought, my father dammed up a much larger reservoir further up the hillside, water from which could have been released into the burn; but as far as I know it never had to be used. This upper reservoir lay at the mouth of a little gorge, with a steep heathery bluff overlooking its upper end; it carried a raft of water-lilies, lent itself to reflections of the bluff and banks when the water was calm, and made a very quiet and private nesting-place for mallard.

The chasm in Glen Skibble was treated in the same way, and with dramatic results. It possessed what were known as a 'Dark Side' and a 'Light Side', the former, on the left bank, being darkened by a heavy growth of Norway spruce and silver fir, while the latter was merely edged with much lighter Scots pine and larch. A guess may be made at the age of the trees as Old Archie MacCallum, who cannot have been born much earlier than 1830, told me that he had worked on the planting. Some of the silver firs, growing at the bottom of the chasm, had made most remarkable growth in their seventy or eighty years, no doubt drawn up to the light from their deeply shaded positions. The Dark Side was partly precipitous and partly a very steep slope encumbered with enormous slabs and lumps of

rock, split, slid and tumbled, and across this face the improvers
had engineered a safe and comfortable footpath, with flights of
stone steps where necessary, ending in a steep descent to the
hollow of Lagan Geoidh. At one point a subsidiary flight of
steps led up from the path to a gazebo – a small platform
enclosed by huge rocks and provided with a stone bench; this
most probably dated from before the planting of the trees, as it
would have given a romantic outlook to the precipice opposite
when the chasm was still clear. Among the rocks above the
gazebo was the 'Hole of the Red Cow' (*Poll na Bo Dearg*), a
cavity in the rocky tumble reached through a smallish opening
and down an underground drop; an exciting place for children,
but actually containing nothing and showing no signs of use.
The small dun described on p.26 stands on its knoll near the
highest point of the path, shortly before the descent to Lagan
Geoidh; the cliff below it is probably the highest and sheerest
in the chasm.

The trees stopped short of the hollow of Lagan Geoidh, a
great scar-bound cup carved out by the burn from a deposit
of red boulder-clay. The left-bank scars were stabilised, being
grown over with turf and bracken, and bearing the beginnings
of the scrub-wood that continued along the burnside up to the
forks. On the right bank, however, the burn curves past the
base of a raw clay cliff, gradually cutting it away; and it is
tempting to suggest that a secondary channel which crosses
the floor of the hollow, as a chord to the main burn's arc,
may have been cut artificially to reduce erosion on the cliff.
Aerial photographs, at any rate, show that the cut is quite
unnaturally straight. The ruins of what must have been the
Wilsons' house (p.62) survived, but no interest attaches to
those of a small, squarish hut, as this was built only about
1895 for use at picnics.

The Light Side of the chasm is largely flanked by precipices,
without slides of fallen rock, and the path has thus been
formed, without engineering, by the ordinary passage of traffic
along the lip. Until recent years, when it was carried away
by a landslip, there was a wishing-well in a rather precarious

position below the path (c.899501), but nothing is left of it today.

One approached the glen by the path built on the former mill-lade, which ran below the kitchen-garden and passed the keeper's house. Both this house and the round so-called 'tower' are older than 1867, though the kennels were built by my father shortly before 1877. My father's keeper, David Coutts, retired about the same time that I began to shoot, his place being taken by his second son Donald, previously the under-keeper. The eldest and youngest sons, Drs David and James Coutts, both practised medicine in Glasgow. The 'tower' was originally a low-standing, roofless enclosure with hutches for ferrets inside it, but at some time it was raised in height, given a conical roof, and used as a store for the keeper's heavy equipment. Some of its contents would rank today as curios, for example, powder-horns for use with muzzle-loading guns, and machines for refilling and recapping spent cartridges. The gunroom was a front parlour in the keeper's house, where the guns were laid out on a table with a green-baize cloth.

The Crow Glen had been less thoroughly improved than the Dark Side of Glen Skibble, but there too a path had been terraced out along the burnside, which was clayey rather than rocky and nowhere precipitous, with wooden bridges and occasional flights of steps. At about the elevation of Caolfin the path left the glen and came out on to a rough heathery field behind the farm, whence walkers could descend by the Light Side of the chasm. The lowermost part of the Crow Glen held an open stand of large sycamore, ash and beech; higher up were larch and Norway spruce of a younger age; and beside the path were some exotic species by which my mother set great store, in particular an extremely vigorous and promising Wellingtonia, and a Cryptomeria japonica. One year a fine Douglas fir developed a double leader, and someone conceived the idea of trimming off the redundant shoot with a bullet; no-one, however, was thought to be a good enough shot except Duncan Campbell of Inverneill, a Bisley marksman, who happened to be staying in the house, and as he had broken his leg it was difficult to get him to the spot. In the end, with great public spirit, he consented to be bumped up the path in an old Bath chair, but nobody was very much surprised when he failed to score. Near the top of the glen the path crossed one of the bloomeries mentioned earlier, and lumps of slag would sometimes work out of the ground and appear on the surface.

Apart from Glen Tuine, on the High Road to Claonaig, the rest of the planted woods were on or about the Home Farm. They provided small timber for fencing and the general needs of the estate, and acted as cover for game and shelter for stock. By my time they were past their best, as the trees had grown too tall to make good cover for pheasants, and rhododendrons were increasing and becoming a pest; they were finally reduced to jungle by the gale of 1911, in which my brother estimated that the estate as a whole lost twenty-nine thousand trees in three quarters of an hour. Subject to these drawbacks, however, they gave a great deal of pleasure, quite apart from their function as coverts, the rides making easy and delightful woodland walks. At their eastern end the coverts ran down to the very rough ground beyond the Point, where they merged with the rocky scrubwoods of the Raised Beach gullies. I remember a thrilling episode on a family walk in this region, when the party halted to admire the view, and someone, wearing a smart Sunday kilt, came within an ace of sitting down in a nest of new-born adders.

My mother was fond of tea-picnics, and also probably found them a useful occupation for guests. The places most favoured were at the Point, in parts of the home coverts, on the Light Side of Glen Skibble, and at Lagan Geoidh. The procedure was for the garden boy to carry the baskets of food, and if necessary a supply of water, to the selected spot in the course of the afternoon; the party, on arrival, then collected the driest sticks that the place afforded, built a fire for the kettle, and duly made tea. Smudge-fires were sometimes needed as well to keep the midges at bay. Unless the place was very distant, we normally carried the empty baskets ourselves on the return journey; I remember how my uncle Henry Hardcastle would carry an empty kettle but nothing larger. Another uncle, Professor George Ramsay, invented a most useful piece of picnic equipment, known as 'the iron stick'. This was a pointed strip, about two inches wide, of stout iron plating, as long as a walking-stick and with a walking-stick's curved handle. The end of the handle was turned up like a retroussé nose; and when the stick was planted by the fire at the correct angle, the kettle could be hung on the turned-up part just clear of the burning embers. This saved all trouble with hearthstones, and the wood could burn undisturbed.

15. GOING OUT TO SHOOT

Winged game, and particularly grouse, probably had a great deal to do with the coming of my family to Skipness in the 1860s. In those days, the possession of a Highland estate was a proper and fashionable ambition for any young man with means, and it was probably for this as well as for other reasons that my father's trustees launched him at the age of eighteen on the career of a Highland proprietor. In those days, of course, the position was less demanding than it later became, when agricultural depression had set in and anti-laird legislation; with the result that a landed proprietor could see as much or as little as he liked of the Highland scene, inviting leisurely friends to shoot grouse or pheasants, or to cruise pleasantly in yachts, and escape to the outer world in the harsher seasons of the year. This was not, of course, the pattern of my own family's life, as we went away from home very little apart from a long visit to London at the end of the winter, to stay with my grandmother, Mrs Hardcastle, and my Monkswell uncle and aunt. (One of these visits coincided with the great frost of 1895, and though I was not yet three at the time I clearly remember the ice-floes drifting up and down the Thames as I watched them from the nursery window at Monkswell House. I had built myself a kind of observation-post, with a high chair and a stuffed elephant's foot.) But though Skipness was far indeed from being a simple plaything, it retained very much the character of a 'sporting estate', and right down to my own time the game and fishing bulked large in everyone's life. Consequently, though accounts of shoots and fishings

103

are the dreariest things in literature, something must be said about them here to make the picture complete.

Shooting can be formal or informal, and as time went on and estates began to look more like business undertakings and less like toys, formality began to give way. The grouse were not primarily affected, as grouse-moors had always to be managed on a regular system. The burning of the heather, for example, had to be intelligently planned, to get rid of big old plants too tall and tough for the birds to browse on, and to secure a proper distribution of fresh young growth in patches of suitable size. At the same time, the tenant of the sheep-farm might have had to be dissuaded from starting big fires at random, and burning as much as he could in vast swathes. Predators had to be discouraged, particularly hoodie crows and greater black-backed gulls, which were interested in eggs and chicks. In my time, again, the practice was to shoot over dogs, and this meant the maintenance of a kennel of setters, idle for most of the year, with attendant problems of breeding, training and exercise. As a result, the party that turned out on a given day, when the season opened, would consist of three, or perhaps only two, guns, with the head keeper to organise proceedings and work the dog, the under-keeper to lead the spare dogs, probably three in number, and carry a game-bag, and in the background a pony, led by yet another man, with panniers for game from the under-keeper's bag. It also carried the lunch, coats and waterproofs, and had to be led with great care to avoid peaty areas, which might bog a pony where a man could pass quite safely. The setters' method of work – quartering the ground, scenting a covey, drawing up slowly towards it with nose levelled and one forefoot raised – has been described so often and depicted with such feeling by numberless Victorian artists that no description is needed here; the guns meanwhile placed themselves behind the dog ready for the covey to burst into the air, when the gun in the middle took the first bird that rose, and the others the outermost birds to right and left.

So far so good in the opening weeks of the season, but only in the opening weeks, for by the time that the birds of the year had come to understand the procedure, and had gained their full strength, they tended to become 'wild', ceased to wait obediently for the dog to give them away, and flew at the first hint of trouble. It was then necessary to fall back on the chancier method of driving, in which several guns were disposed in a line of butts and the grouse were driven over them by a force of beaters. In the days to which these reminiscences mainly refer, the driving of grouse at Skipness was rather a haphazard business, though in later years my brother devoted a great deal of thought and effort to improving the tactics. There were several reasons why driving was less easy than it looked. In the first place, the birds' own views and habits had to be known, and attention paid to them in laying plans for the drives, as it was useless to attempt to drive them where they would firmly refuse to go. Then the butts had to be sited where guns could see the birds approaching, without the birds seeing the guns and swerving aside. Beaters had to be obtained, at a season when surplus men were apt to be employed on the harvest, and had to be kept marching in some kind of an orderly line. Flankers had to be posted at selected points, to turn birds back if they tried to swing away, and to do so without scaring everything back where it had come from. Ideally the birds disturbed in the earlier drives should have ended up on ground from which they could have been driven back later in the day, crossing the same butts from another direction; but for this the lie of the land at Skipness was not particularly favourable, the birds being able to fly off, as it were at a tangent, instead of being shuttled to and fro across a concavity. So complex an operation was only attempted once or twice in the season, and grouse-shooting thus rapidly lost its formality when autumn began; thereafter the guns and keeper simply walked the hill in line, visiting likely spots and picking up such birds as failed to get away in time.

My own experience of these shoots relates only to the northern part of the estate, as the rest was ordinarily let, with Claonaig Lodge. The northern beats were Monybackach, Laggan, Altagalvash and the so-called 'High Beat', this last a distant and rather unproductive area above Glenskibble. The first two were the easiest to reach and the least strenuous to walk, and also held the most birds. A favourite place for having lunch was near the top of the Monybackach hill, where an iron-tasting spring bubbled up the side of a moss, and the remains of the roots and trunks of ancient trees appeared out of the peat. The lunches themselves were rather prosaic affairs, consisting of cold-meat sandwiches made in the kitchen, and pieces of cake. The drinks were uninspiring too by modern standards, as vacuum flasks had not yet been invented; there was probably a supply of whisky and some bottles of soda water, with unbreakable metal tumblers, and people quite often drank the iron spring. The soda water bottles would be of great interest today, being of very thick glass, with pointed bottoms like amphorae, and sealed with stoppers in the form of a glass marble; to get at the contents, this marble had to be pressed inwards, down the neck of the bottle with a patent wooden opener, the inside of the neck being so shaped as to catch and hold the marble, preventing it from blocking the flow. Nobody thought of tea, though at this distance of time the gap between a sandwich lunch and a seven-thirty dinner, with no prospect of sherry before it, looks like an aching void. And I remember how, on one occasion, some rather weak vessel had to be revived with hot soup when he came in about six o'clock in a state approaching collapse.

Clothes have probably changed less than foods and drinks, as they were dictated by unchanging conditions of weather and terrain. In the wet a kilt was probably better than knickerbockers, as the latter were apt to cling round the knees like cold compresses in prolonged rain. Everyone made a point of wearing stout, hand-made stockings, in the knitting of which female relatives performed prodigies. In respect of footwear, there were two schools of thought - those who believed that heavy boots would keep the feet dry all day, and those who expected to get wet whatever they wore and thought it better to squelch the water in and out, from light brogues, rather than to macerate their feet in waterlogged boots.

It must have been the pheasants that first noticed informality creeping in. In the earlier and more spacious days, eggs had been collected from the fatuous pheasant mothers and entrusted to experienced hens, which had hatched them out and nursed the young birds safely through their infancy and chickhood. Every summer a colony of coops had had to be formed, with a portable wired-in run in front of each, the position of the colony being changed year by year on a seven-year cycle to avoid infection with 'the gapes'; and when the young birds were thought to be old enough to manage their own lives they had been turned out into the coverts to wait for October. But at that point formal methods began to give way, as the most intelligent and adaptable birds tended not to wait but to leak out of the coverts on to the adjoining moorland, where they could find all sorts of insects, seeds and small berries, and delicious ants' larvae for the scratching. In fact, they copied the grouse, as renegade Normans in Ireland copied the native chieftains, and when they had lived down the convention of going up to roost in trees, as they could safely do as foxes and wild cats were unknown in Kintyre, they were virtually lost to the system of formal covert-shoots. Nor, for that matter, were the coverts well adapted for the classical pheasant *battue*, providing few stands where guns could expect a satisfactory stream of high birds, while frequently allowing the pheasants, which are splendid natural runners, to outdistance the beaters and make their escape sideways. The attempt to show pheasants as they might have been shown on a well-ordered English estate was largely given up in the early years of this century, and with it the business of raising young birds artificially under barn-door hens. The 'wild' stock was quite able to keep itself going on a scale sufficient for rough winter shooting, when the birds could be roused out of cover by a single man and a dog.

The bag in a winter shoot was generally light but mixed, and might include pheasants, blackgame, woodcock and snipe, with perhaps a grouse or a wood-pigeon. Blackgame were still plentiful at the beginning of the century, and in winter gathered in the scrubwoods to browse on the buds of the birch trees. Half-a-dozen great black birds make a very odd spectacle sitting in the crown of a small, stunted tree like a crop of enormous berries. In the upper part of Glen Skibble they could sometimes be driven in a really spectacular way. A beater, or perhaps a sister with Pepper, the family terrier, would make a circuitous approach to the higher gullies of the western branch of the burn, put up the birds from the scrub, and start them on a course down the main part of the glen or across to its eastern flank. They came over very high, and with a strong west wind behind them could no doubt have been making some sixty miles an hour by the time they reached the guns posted in the main glen. Their size and speed were all the more impressive at a time when great machines had not yet begun to tear about the sky. The sea-face beyond Altagalvash was another favourite place, but here one usually had to take a 'snap' shot among the scrubby oaks and birches, while trying not to slip into some rocky cleft or pitfall. At harvest time the blackgame came down into the fields, with pheasants and a few grouse, to feed on the stooked oats, and could be stalked with a smallbore rifle; but such stalks were rarely successful, as the birds were extremely wary, particularly the grouse, which seemed to know that they were out of place in a field and were always the first to go. The blackgame would stay for a very few seconds longer, but the pheasants were rather slow in understanding that something was wrong. I only once saw blackcocks performing in a so-called 'lek'; the affair was staged in the middle of the day, not in the early morning, but in other respects followed the bird-book rules, the cock birds cooing and making a great display, and the greyhen spectators registering a total lack of interest.

The woodcock were partly home-bred and partly migrants, but I never remember a big flock of migrants appearing when they were hoped for, namely with the full moon of November. What brought them into the coverts, of course, was frost on the more open ground, and the same brought down the snipe from the hill to unfrozen mosses and ponds. The so-called

Snipe Pond just outside the front garden nearly always held at least one snipe even in open weather. As a final tribute to the woodcock I feel bound to record, admittedly in despite of much learned opinion, that I once myself saw an old bird fly away carrying a nestling; it was clutched between her thighs, and her legs were hanging down in a thoroughly distinctive way.

Our hares were of the Blue species, which turns white in winter and is dreadfully conspicuous in a district where snow is so rare. They were not confined to ground above a thousand feet, and were often picked up in the course of an ordinary grouse-shoot.

Underlying nobler game there was always, of course, the rabbit. Myxomatosis was still far in the future, and rabbits swarmed like bees. A keeper and an under-keeper, and sometimes a trapper as well, worked at them year in and year out with guns and snares, but still they continued to swarm. The trapper may perhaps have been rather a mixed blessing, as his personal interest would undoubtedly have been to leave some modest stock to breed him his next year's job; and the farmers, too, probably failed to understand quite how much grass the rabbits were taking out of the mouths of their sheep, and tended, quite wrongly, to regard sales of rabbits as profit. In any case, some rabbits must be thought of as forming part of every bag secured on the lower-lying ground, and for that matter many rabbits lived right out on the heather, as if they were trying to be deer. On occasion the keepers used ferrets, but this might be a chilly and often a frustrating business, if the ferret, instead of driving the rabbit out, killed it in the burrow and then settled down to a juicy meal underground.

The Claonaig beats, as I have said, were usually let, along with the winter shooting in Claonaig Glen and in the scrubwoods on the coast to the south. The tenants lived in Claonaig Lodge, overlooking the steep, mossy slope that fell to burn and its haugh-lands, and with the oaks and birches of the scrubwoods growing right up to the windows. This house was something of an architectural portent, as it had begun its career long before as a prefabricated wooden building, the parts of which had come over from Norway by sea and were landed somewhere on the beach. The corrugated iron roof was probably an original feature, though the iron sheathing of the walls may perhaps have been added to suit the West Highland climate. It was T-shaped on plan, and was originally guaranteed to last for twenty-five years; but in fact it survived intact until quite recent times. It suffered from several drawbacks as a place of residence, including – oddly, with a rainfall of fifty-odd inches – a thoroughly defective water-supply; heavy rain, too, drumming on the roof, produced a deafening noise, while the inside was haunted by a most peculiar smell, which no measures could eradicate. The wooded glen, however, was a place of great beauty, with wild flowers of every kind.

16. TROUT

I learned to fish, at least with a worm, in the small burn immediately behind the House. It was said in the family that fish never came to anyone before he was five, and this was pretty certainly true in my own case. I retain a mental picture of my first fish, flapping on the end of the line, but cannot reconstruct the circumstances of his capture. The only pool on that burn that was worth the expenditure of a worm was just by the back door; it might hold a brown trout of up to five ounces in weight. No sea-trout had ever been known to force his way up to this very small stream even in the most violent spates, but one could always hope. Regrettably there were also eels, small but able to twist up one's line into an awful slimy tangle, and an eel was in fact the only probable reward for trying other pools higher up. Worms for this phase of the sport were dug from the leafmould dump in the front garden, and were carried, with a wisp of fresh grass, in the small tins in which pipe-tobacco was marketed, with airholes punched in the lids. One was morally bound to release unused worms at the end of the day, and above all things not to leave deposits of old worms to fester in the pockets of coats which might be worn by one's elders.

Though familiarised, in these ways, from an early age with the niceties of the local fishings, I never became a devout or really skilful fisherman in the class of my brother or my cousin Owen O'Malley. I thus hardly feel justified in attempting to write this chapter, the more so as my taste in fishing was certainly debased in later life through catching too many big fish too easily. I confess to having felt no scruple in catching big

Arctic char, in Canadian lakes, with cubes of pork cast in the manner of a fly, and representing, I suppose, to the fish carrion gobbets dropped by crows or ospreys; or in taking salmon and cod turn about when trolling in salt water with a copper-wire trace. However, in the years to which these memories refer, I was still fishing the Skipness burn with diligence, as well as paying occasional visits to the lochs which were inconveniently distant before the coming of motor transport. Claonaig burn was usually let to tenants, and I never came to know much about it.

As I remember the Skipness burn, there were three pools in or near the village where anyone could catch a sea-trout, if the water was in the right condition, or a brown trout of more than half a pound, and where the experts might do very much better; there was also one doubtful pool, where an expert might sometimes get something, and two more which were spoken of vaguely as having once held fish. The first of the certainties was a deep, thunderous hole at the lower end of the chasm, with a fall at its head and a rock-bound rapid higher up; this place was impossible to fish while a spate was at its height, but it remained in condition after the shallower pools had run down and cleared. We used to watch the sea-trout hurling themselves up the fall, and sometimes eels slithering up the wet rock-faces alongside. The next was a short distance downstream, at the tail of the island, where the junction of the two streams made an interesting place for the larger fish to lie. The third was the best pool on the burn, a long curving run by the southern end of Strathbuie, its further bank revetted with wooden posts and held together by the roots of small bushy alders. These alders were sometimes troublesome, making it hard for the unwary to place their casts without getting caught up on a twig. The pool of rather doubtful value was opposite the post office, and has now disappeared as the burn has lately formed its new mouth at this point. The so-called pools where endeavour was always lost were a shallow expanse by the curve in the village street, and the tidal stretch at the burn's former mouth; the theory was that if a grilse happened to be looking round, the tidal stretch would be the likeliest place to meet him, but in fact the larger the fly that one exhibited here, the smaller the fish that took it.

In addition to these pools near home, there were the so-called 'upper pools', on the distant stretch between Lagan Geoidh and the forks. The most distant of these, a large, deep pot below a waterfall, had been known to produce sea-trout of up to three pounds, generally early in the season; it was thought that the fall was too high for even the big fish to leap, and that this pool marked the head of sea-trout navigation. The remainder of the upper pools might sometimes reward an expert, but the beat as a whole was not particularly attractive. At one point the burn rushed violently through a rocky crevice, almost a tunnel below but topped by a slit which seemed narrow enough to step over; the place was called 'the Stride', but whether anyone ever actually bestrode it is more than I can say.

The only loch at the 'home' end of the estate was Loch na Machrach Moire (p.4), and this was useless for fishing as no stock of trout could maintain itself, for lack of places to spawn. The loch itself was peaty, and it possessed no tributary streamlet. My father introduced some small trout on at least one occasion, but none of them was ever seen again – unless, no doubt, by herons and red-throated divers. Before the days of motor transport, Loch Crinne was the only good fishing-loch that was at all easy of access, and even that called for a bicycle-ride to Glenreasdell and a two-mile walk beyond. We kept a boat on Loch Crinne, and used to catch fair bags of rather small brown trout, though in later years, when motor bicycles and cars made heavier fishing possible, the size of the fish improved. No sea-trout seems ever to have reached Loch Crinne, though a very small stream runs down into the Claonaig Burn.

Of the group of lochs at the south-western end of the estate – Loch Romain, Loch an Eilein, Lochan a' Chreimh, Lochan Fraoich – I knew very little myself, but Loch an Eilein had the reputation of holding some good-sized fish. Mrs Higginson gives it a story, illustrating the value of a darning-needle stuck in the bonnet, or of a dog, but not of a bitch, in repelling ghosts and fairies. She writes as follows of a handloom weaver called Mackintosh, who lived at Eascairt:

> He was coming home late at night from Clachan direction. Nothing could frighten him he was wearing a broad blue bonnet with the customary darning needle stuck inside it and his dog accompanied him. When he was crossing over at Loch nan Eilain he met a very tall man and Mackintosh spoke to him. Of course it was a spectre. He asked the spectre where would he find an oolly (*ulaidh*, treasure). The spectre answered him if it was not for the darning needle you have in your bonnet and that pup of a dog you have with you I would oolly you. The man took that answer as threatening to himself but anyway the spectre did not harm him.

Another loch, called Loch an t'Saoir Carridh after the 'joiner Kerr' who was the subject of the following story, once existed somewhere east of Garveorine but has now disappeared, evidently as a result of drainage. Of Kerr, Mrs Higginson writes:

> He was living in Strone; one moonlight night he was going across to Lagavullin (the inn at Redhouse) another man accompanied him. When they came to the lochside they met a horse and this man Kerr thought he wanted to take this horse and ride him so he got on the horse's back, the other man returning home to Strone. Well Kerr reached Lagavullin so the story goes and left again for home riding the horse. His body was found at the side of the loch next morning very much mangled and torn but the horse was never seen or heard of before or after that night. This was no doubt a witch in the shape of a horse.

Water-horses were, of course, one of the most dangerous things that anyone could meet in the Highlands.

17. FARMS AND CROFTS

Archibald Campbell, the first Campbell laird of Skipness, received his charter from his father, the second Earl of Argyll, in 1511. This instrument mentions some names which are clearly the same as those of later farms on the estate, others which are recognisable but which are now outside its boundaries, and others again which cannot be identified at all. On the present estate are Origage (Oragaig), Craggane (Creggan), Clynage (Claonaig), Glenrysadill (Glenreasdell), Strone Garfoling (Garveorine), Cullentraithe (Culindrach), Aireoure (Ariour), Escardy (Eascairt), Skippinnych (Skipness), Glenskippail (Glenskibble), Kilpayne (presumably Caolfin). Now outside are Roage (Lagganroig), Airmore and Kynnacraig (Kennacraig), Bereddirtnaawin (Bardaravine), Achequhois (Achahoish); while nothing is known to correspond with Achingerrin and Auchindownwoll (Achtydownegall in 1481 and Auchintydonald in 1549). The foregoing names correspond almost exactly with those in the Earl's own charter, of 1502, and in Sir Duncan Forestare's, of 1495, except that both these latter contain in addition Le Altgallereas (Altagalvash), while Eascairt and Skipness are omitted. 'Lethourlee et Kilelee' (1495) and 'Lathourling et Kilpenny' (1502) should probably not be associated with Caolfin, as the resemblance of Kilpenny to Kilpayne seems slight and Kilpayne itself is not certainly Caolfin. A charter of 1481, to the Lord of the Isles, mentions Tescard (Eascairt), Gartwaich (Gartavaich) and Owragag (Oragaig) together with Altbeith and Scottomyl (Scotmill), now no longer on the estate. In much later times, a valuation roll of 1751 lists Altagalvash, Altbeith, Ariour, Caolfin, Claonaig, Creggan, Culindrach, Eascairt, Garveorine, Glenreasdell, Glenskibble, Lagganroig, Oragaig, Skipness (with mill), and Strone.

Beyond proving a certain continuity in the organisation of the farms over a period of at least three centuries, these lists do comparatively little to advance the present subject; but the conditions that obtained at the turn of the eighteenth and nineteenth centuries deserve a closer look. The wind of agricultural improvement was evidently blowing through Argyll as early as the 1770s, as the fifth Duke reorganised his farms in 1779, substituting enclosed units, with enterprising tenants, for the old runrig holdings, and starting new crofting and fishing villages for surplus tenants removed from the land in the process. A recent writer has said that there thus emerged in Kintyre a society comprising tenant farmers, farm-workers, and a disproportionately large class of cottars. Among the Duke's 'enterprising tenants' there were no doubt immigrants from Ayrshire or descendants of earlier incomers of Lowland stock, bearing for example such names as Cook, Taylor, Wilson or Thomson, as a 'Plantation' of Kintyre with Lowlanders had begun in 1607 with the foundation of a burgh at Campbeltown, and had been given further impetus, particularly at Saddel, in the 1650s and later. The depopulation caused by the Macdonald raid of 1645 (p.40) and its aftermath, which included an epidemic of plague, together with the depredations of Athol's troops after Argyll's rebellion in 1685, must likewise have left much land open for colonisation.

At Skipness, by 1794, 'improvement' had made some progress, as the minister could write, in the *Statistical Account*, of enclosure, planting and some recently built farm-houses. Regular rotation of crops was also practised on the best ground. Among drawbacks to progress he mentions the high cost of fuel and manure, the prevalence of too-short leases, and a plethora of small tenants; and some of these drawbacks had apparently not been overcome even fifty years later, when the *New Statistical Account* provides some further evidence. Thus, taking one parish with another, it would seem that in 1843 farm leases were given for nineteen, nine or seven years, but in many cases only from year to year, and that small, uneconomic holdings were a serious social evil. On this the minister of the neighbouring parish of Kilcalmonell and Kilberry writes:

> The landholders . . . have lent their sanction, from time immemorial, to the establishment of a cottage and village system over their estates. The farm is let to a tenant at a given rent, and he is subjected to no conditions as to the management. He has cottagers at two or three places on his farm; each of whom engages to pay rent of from £2 to £5 per annum;

and he goes on to deplore the consequent loss of ambition among the cottars, their frequent recourse to illicit distillation to find the money for their rent, and the multiplication of paupers. He is particularly hard on the smugglers, of whom more will be said later, opining that it is 'impossible to calculate the amount of evil that this unholy and unpatriotic traffic is the cause of'.

An idea of conditions on the farms is given by Lord Teignmouth's description, of 1836. 'The farmhouses', he writes,

> are . . . far behind the general improvement visible in this part of the country. The entrance is usually through the byre, which is a continuation of the house in the same line: the fire is placed in the middle of the floor, contained in a grate, either square like a bowl, and raised a little above the ground, a custom peculiar to Cantyre. They are without lofts, probably as the country furnishes no poles, and are cold, as the thatched roof forms their only covering . . . The cottages in Cantyre are generally respectable, and the cottars usually have kail-yards and pasture for a cow, but there is a marked distinction between them and the farm-houses. Fifty years ago, before the improvements commenced, the houses of the farmers were on a footing with the poorest of the present cottagers.

The kinds of improvement actually in progress in 1843 in the parish of Saddell and Skipness were the reclamation of wastes, the introduction of manuring and draining, and the proper rotation of crops. In addition, the minister records the 'erection of subdivided farms into one', by which he presumably means the enclosure and consolidation of runrig multiple tenancies; he gives this as one of the causes of a decrease in the population, another cause being the taking-over of farms into the laird's own hands. Figures which he quotes show that in 1821 the parish had 2191 inhabitants, risen from 1360 in 1755, that in 1831 it still had 2152, but in 1841 only 1748. This suggests that although Robert Campbell is shown by his wife's diaries to have been an enthusiastic improver, such rationalisations as he effected among the cottars and crofters can hardly have been very drastic, as the period of his activity (1807-14) coincided with that of the highest population; again, Mrs Campbell's note that, on the day in 1813 when the laird's peats were brought home, 'between in and out of door devourers we had no less than 152 people to feed', points to a mob of small men supplying customary services.

Though the figure for the population of the parish as a whole had dropped before the end of the Campbell regime at Skipness, it may well not reflect the impact of modernisation on the estate of Skipness itself. In point of fact, blame for the hardships that followed reorganisation is placed by local tradition on the shoulders of William Fraser, the elder laird of that name. It is true that between 1814, when Robert Campbell died, and 1843, when Fraser came in, there was ample time for reforms to have been introduced; but no stories were told about evictions by Walter Campbell, Robert's son, or of crofts or kailyards being taken to form centralised farms, or for the change from cattle to sheep. Fraser, on the other hand, appears to have introduced methods which were currently in use in the Lowlands without regard for local needs and conditions, and whatever he did earned him such bitter hatred that after his death stones were thrown at his coffin. The fact that several smallholdings beside the High Road, a short distance west of the village, were already ruinous in 1867 may well point to a clearance of crofters or cottars from this area, and it is worth noting that one of the holdings, Bailean-cleirich, was said by Mrs Higginson to have been inhabited about 1800. The people said to have been removed from behind the village (p.53) might, on this analogy, have been cottars on Caolfin farm. Once made, Fraser's arrangements seem to have persisted without material change, though my grandmother and father enlarged or improved most or all of the farm-houses. The subdivision of the House Farm with drystone dykes was pretty certainly Fraser's work.

The farms and cottages as they existed about 1900, and some abandoned sites possessing a history as farms, may be conveniently described as follows, together with their folklore as preserved by Mrs Higginson. The list is arranged topographically from north to south.

Ariour. Charters of 1495 and later; Robert Gordon's map of c.1640. In my time a ruin. According to Mrs Higginson, a 'treasure' (*ulaidh*) was believed to have been found here early in the nineteenth century.

Altagalvash. Charters of 1495 and later. In 1502 Altagalvash and Ariour together amounted to two merklands. On Robert Gordon's map. In my time a shepherd's house, inhabited by Donald MacLellan, who made splendid crook-handled walking-sticks. For shipment to market, the wool from this part of the hill had to be moved by boat from the bay below the shepherd's house to the pier, about a mile distant. Mrs Higginson has a story about a flying serpent, which settled near Altagalvash at some time in the seventeenth century, and killed cattle and sheep. It was killed by a very brave man called Thomson, who, however, died of its poison twenty years later, when he cut himself fingering the old rust on his sword.

Culindrach. Charters of 1495 and later (two merklands); marked on Robert Gordon's map, and shown as a group of houses on Roy's map (1747-55). If it is true that the laird's family lived here for a time at the turn of the seventeenth and eighteenth centuries, they certainly did not inhabit the existing house, as this is evidently of fairly recent construction.

Cnocandonn. A group of cottages facing Culindrach across a small burn, one of them showing provision for a cruck-trussed roof. Though ruinous by 1900, one of the houses was inhabited by a tailor as lately as the 1880s.

Old Pier. A double house, presumably built in association with the harbour. One house was occupied by the Hyndmans, and the other by the Misses Armour, who worked the smallholding.

Puirt a' Chruidh. Ruined houses standing on a bluff above the landing-place. A valuation roll of 1855 shows three tenants, which suggests that this was a runrig holding later absorbed in the Home Farm.

Laggan. This place, marked as a group of houses on Roy's map, was last inhabited about 1882 and its remains have now been entirely removed. It occupied a charming site by a small burn, in a sheltered hollow, and was passed by the old road that is marked on the OS map of 1867 as running on to Cnocandonn and Culindrach. Mrs Higginson believed that treasure had been hidden at Laggan, and also records a dubious piece of folklore. 'Malcolm McQuilkan', she writes,

> lived at Laggan he was a shoemaker to trade, he was a very queer man in his way he got the idea if he had two wings he could fly in a good breeze of wind. So he made two round wooden hoops and covered them with sheepskins (these articles were called fasgags) and sewed a lot of feathers all round them. On a very windy day he went up on the top of his house and tried to fly and fell down in the ash-pit.

This story however bears a suspicious resemblance to Bishop Lesley's account of what happened to the Abbot of Tongland, a man 'of curious ingyne' and a protégé of James IV. Bishop Lesley writes that he

> tuik in hand to flie with wingis . . . and to that effect he causet mak ane pair of wingis of fedderis, quhilkis beand fessinit apoun him he flew of the castell wall of Striveling [Stirling], bot schortlie he fell to the ground and brak his thee bane; bot the wyt thairof he asscryvit to that thair was sum hen fedderis in the wingis, quhilk yarnit and covet the mydding and not the skyis.

Monybackach. This farm was worked by the Misses Armour, after they had removed from the Old Pier. Nothing about its origin is on record, but it preserves, jointly with Laggan, a good example of a turf-built 'head-dyke' designed to separate the hill grazings from the 'outfields' of the old unimproved farms. This dyke runs along the face of the hill above both farms between the three hundred feet and four hundred feet contours, and is associated with a wide, dyked passage, debouching at Monybackach, by which animals could have been driven through the belt of cultivated land. The passage no doubt served also for whatever pack-horses and sledges brought peat down from the hags on the higher ground.

Home Farm. Some kind of home farm, for the supply of the Castle, is presumably indicated by the entry Skippinnych (four merklands) in the charter of 1511, while in later times the Castle itself appears to have been organised, or re-organised, for farming purposes shortly before 1794 (p.40). As has been said, the Home Farm was probably laid out in its present form by William Fraser. The existing farm-steading was built new by my father on a virgin site when he cleared the Castle courtyard. The shepherd at the steading was Duncan MacLellan, brother of Donald at Altagalvash, and like him famous as a maker of crook-handled sticks.

Caolfin. Probably represented by Kilpayne (two merklands) in the charter of 1511. Marked on Robert Gordon's map of c.1640, and as a group of houses, though on the wrong side of Glen Skibble, on Roy's map of 1747-55. Like other settlements so marked, it was probably analogous with the 'ferm-touns' of the Lowlands, in which case the presence here of the tailor whose tombstone appears in the graveyard, or at Laggan of the shoemaker mentioned by Mrs Higginson, would be fully explained. It was tenanted by one Munro, who doubled as blacksmith in the village; he was said to have been a good piper, but gave up the pipes under the influence of Christian Endeavour.

Glenskibble. Charters of 1495 and later (one and two merklands); Robert Gordon's map; valuation rolls of 1751.

Mrs Robert Campbell mentions the place as a farm in 1813, but by the later years of the century it had become a shepherd's house and it has now been totally removed. Wool and heavy loads used to go in and out over the very rough track on a vehicle known as a slype, that is to say a sledge with its runners formed of the curved butt-ends of the shafts.

Goirteaneorna. A small farm, not appearing in the early records and perhaps formed by Fraser through the amalgamation of some neighbouring crofts shown as ruins on the OS map of 1867 – Auchanandunan, Eascahadhu, Bailean-cleirich. The tenants were named Cook.

Glenbuie. A small farm not mentioned in the early records. Mrs Higginson places here a version of the familiar story of a woman who gets involved with fairies, dances with them all night and finds her shoes worn out in the morning.

Achameanach. Not mentioned in the earlier records but marked on Roy's map of 1747-55.

High Claonaig. Not a farm, but mentioned by Mrs Higginson as a place where a man called Archibald Hyndman fell in with a large number of fairies. They 'convoyed him to the top of the old road above Skipness, they playing the bagpipes and chattering to one another but they never interfered with the man'.

Claonaig Inn. The farm associated with Claonaig Inn at the end of the nineteenth century no doubt represented the Clyneagir, Clynaig, Clynage and Clonak of the charters; this is marked by Robert Gordon c.1640, and by Roy, who shows a group of houses. The Inn itself is marked on the OS map of 1867 as close to the church but on the right bank of the small burn, and the existing farmhouse, which was licensed as an inn until well after the turn of the century, must have been built since 1867 by my grandmother or father. The last holder of the licence was Neil Currie, and after his death the farm was taken on by Peter Campbell, gamekeeper for the Claonaig portion of the estate.

Mrs Higginson has a story about doings at Claonaig Inn which seems less unlikely than much of her other material.

A man named Peter MacMillan formerly kept the Inn, and one day, when both of them were drunk, he bought the wife of John Menzies, his opposite number from the inn that then functioned at Skipness. Menzies went home, got sober, and forgot the whole transaction, but MacMillan duly turned up in his best clothes and with a pillion saddle on his horse, demanding delivery of the wife. The wife, now hearing of the business for the first time, was understandably annoyed with her husband, and

> It was said that she thrashed him up and down the village until his clothes were in tatters. She did not go away with MacMillan, but she had a small room built at the back of the house for herself. It was said that she never ate nor slept with her husband after that, also that she never forgave him for selling her to Peter MacMillan.

In the section of her work devoted to witches and witchcraft, Mrs Higginson writes, with sharply pointed discretion. 'A few of them that practised the art was resident in Claonaig Glen'.

Glenreasdell Mains. Glenreasdell (two merklands) appears, variously spelt, in the charters of 1495, 1502 and 1511, on Gordon's map of c.1640, and again on Roy's map of 1747-55. The last shows it as two adjoining groups of houses, and the Claonaig Burn is named after it 'Water of Glenreasdale.' Violence was done to tradition, however, when the late Sir Peter Mackie bought the land, then part of Stonefield estate, built himself a new house near Whitehouse, and named this 'Glenreasdell', distinguishing the original Glenreasdell by adding the uncharacteristic Lowland 'Mains'. The farm was subsequently let to the late Ronald Ker, younger of Dougalston, who made local history by owning the first car in the district. It had only one cylinder, and its top speed on the flat was thirty miles an hour. His dog Sammy could keep up with it for moderate distances.

Gartavaigh. Like Glenreasdell, Gartavaigh was acquired by Mackie from Stonefield, and was then, as far as I know, no more than a shepherd's house. It figures, however, in the Skipness charters of 1481, 1568 and 1620, in the last with the mention of a mill, and is marked on Robert Gordon's map of c.1640.

Strone and Garveorine. Both these places are named in the early charters, each as a farm of one merkland, and in the late nineteenth century they were still inhabited by shepherds. The former name is given as 'Stronerestill' in 1495 and 1502, and on Roy's map this place is a group of houses, comparable with the ones at the nearby Glenreasdell.

Creggan. Craggane or Craiggane is mentioned in the charters of 1511 (two merklands) and 1549, and is shown on Roy's map as a group of houses; but its position in Roy's day was half a mile to the west, beside the track that ran down the south-west side of Claonaig Glen (p.16).

Rockfield. This small holding is not mentioned in the charters, but its obviously English name may have replaced one of the vanished Gaelic ones mentioned on p.115. The house, roofless by 1966, was once the scene of a painful domestic crisis. The crofter's wife was confined, and the birth had just been safely accomplished when the local skilly woman who had acted as midwife fell down in one of the epileptic fits to which she was unhappily prone. The patient leaped out of bed, and rushed up the hill to Creggan to summon help, climbing over fences and dykes. In the long run nobody seems to have been any the worse.

Oragaig. Charters of 1481 and later (four merklands); Gordon's map of c.1640 and Roy's of 1747-55. In 1495 the name has the form 'Orgagir', which recalls the 'Clyneagir' used at the same date for Claonaig. This neighbourhood seems to have been particularly dangerous by reason of the fairies who infested it. Mrs Higginson writes, of a wood between Oragaig and Creggan, that 'it was namely for fairies and ghosts, and strong-minded men fought shy of passing through it at night'. A man called Gilbert Taylor had an unpleasant experience here:

One night when he was about the middle of the wood he heard talking and a great noise coming behind he left the road and let them pass they were riding on wee white ponies. Men and women wee wee things all dressed in green and so numerous all speaking Gaelic. They dismounted beside him and he took to his heels with fright they following him and shouting one to another Stop him up and stop him down, and drive him up to the Ear Hill. However, he got away from them . . .

Again, an Oragaig woman was taken away by the fairies and kept for seven years; but she was ultimately rescued by her husband, who managed to break the spell by waylaying the fairy cavalcade and throwing her wedding-dress over her as she went past. Another woman once found the heather on the hill above Oragaig covered with gold pieces; she went for bags to carry them away, but when she returned to the place everything had vanished. Warnings of deaths, too, might be seen or heard; William Fraser's death, for example, was foretold by fires which burned without leaving any mark on the ground, and the sound of a horse trotting was heard at the place where the minister subsequently fell off his horse and was killed. A holly-tree which danced in the road, preventing a certain woman from going up to her house, was classed by Mrs Higginson as 'another bit of witchcraft'.

Eascairt. This was probably the Tescard of 1481 and the Escarde (one merkland) of 1511; but, as the latter grant includes several places on West Loch Tarbert, its Escarde may possibly be the Escart near Tarbert. It is marked on Roy's map of 1747-55. The farm was held for many years by Charles Maclean, brother of Peter Maclean, my father's factor. It was said that Charles, when sixteen years old, was teaching Latin to the younger boys in the school.

18. A HUNDRED YEARS

I remember how a woman once said, of a draft of recruits who had joined my regiment in Haddington, 'Responsibility is staampit on their faces'. Enough has been said in earlier chapters to suggest that late-Victorian Skipness, with its well-kept houses, passable road, regular steamer service and two rival churches, fully qualified for the same kind of tribute; but a doubt remains as to whether its respectable life was as interesting to live as that of its Georgian forerunner. Mrs Robert Campbell and Mrs Higginson both suggest, in their different ways, that here, as elsewhere, a good deal was lost with the disappearance of unregenerate farming, traditional crafts and general freedom from dependence on the outer world.

One quality, for example, of the older community which emerges from Mrs Higginson's notes is its vigour in social activities. Such things as weddings and funerals were given the amplest treatment. 'Their weddings', Mrs Higginson writes, 'generally lasted a week', and great numbers of friends and neighbours were intimately involved. The affair would begin on a Friday night, with a ceremony called 'bottling' in Mrs Higginson's English. This consisted of a visit by the man to his prospective bride's house, to find out whether her parents would accept him into the family; if they were not willing to do so, 'someone would pin the dishcloth to the tail of his coat as that was the signal to depart' – just as in the ballad of 'Jeannie's Bawbee' – but, 'this was very seldom done as they were nearly all relations, cousins marrying cousins'. If the 'bottling' passed off safely, the pair would be proclaimed in Claonaig Church

on the Sunday, or if there was no service on that day some of
the neighbours would be called to the church door, where the
session clerk would make the proclamation. The wedding-day
would be the Tuesday of the same week, and 'they would keep
the sport up all the week, finishing off on the Sunday after the
wedding with the "kirkin"' – this last perhaps at Carradale or
Clachan if the minister had to be searched for. In these cases
'they walked in couples with one or two pipers in front, they
used to dance in some parts on the way and set up a foursome
reel. It used to be a very merry time until the Kirkin was over,
when the young folks were classed with the old folks'. The
wedding evidently called for a tremendous feast, presumably
on the Tuesday:

> Every married woman would go to the house of the bride's
> parents with presents, hens and ducks butter cheese eggs and
> loads of oat cakes. The day before the wedding the women
> would be baking and peeling potatoes and plucking hens,
> maybe 30 or 40 hens would be put into large pots and boilers
> to cook and to have ready, and the potatoes would be mashed
> with rolls of butter.

Of funerals, similarly, she writes:

> Every man young and old would go to a funeral. They used
> to sit up every night, a number of people taking turn about of
> sitting up a wake in a goodly way, the group of men and women
> would take turn about of reading the Bible and singing psalms.
> On the day of the funeral all the relatives would gather in from
> far and near, men and women, and after the funeral was over
> all the neighbours would go back to the house of mourning
> to sympathise with the bereaved . . . When there was a death
> in any of the townships nobody would do any work out of
> respect to the deceased until the funeral was over.

In strong contrast to these works of communal amity was the
anti-social and highly deleterious activity of the witches. Mrs
Higginson evidently believed firmly in witchcraft, alleging that
'some of the art was in vogue' in the parish as recently as twelve
years before the time at which she was writing, that is to say, in

the last decade of the nineteenth century. She seems to have had certain actual people in mind, as in another passage she excuses herself from naming any names on the ground that descendants of a witch were still living in the neighbourhood. The Skipness witches seem to have shown little originality, their art having been restricted to such commonplace things as taking milk from cows, or cream from churns, or 'the virtue' from the whisky in the days of the smuggling, or in one case drowning a fisherman. This last was thought to have been done by a certain Ann Mackillop, who had been 'drummed out of Mull' for witchcraft and with whom the fisherman had been so unwise as to quarrel on the subject of her niece Janet. His boat foundered on a windless day in summer, both the man and his brother being lost; subsequently their father tried to destroy Ann's powers by catching her and cutting her petticoat, but whether this treatment was effective or not has not been recorded. Ann MacKillop may well have been a hard case as she went in heavily for cats. 'She would never drown any kittens. They were as thick as bees about her house and she had beds for the cats all over the house, and it would be a pity of the man woman or child who would illuse or thrown a stone at the cats'. One woman defeated a witch who had been taking her cows' milk by the well-known pin-sticking method, which she learned from

> someone on the Largieside who had the knowledge . . . At sundown she made all the house secure by blocking all doors and closing the windows also closing every hole and crannie even to the keyholes she put on a roaring fire she took a three-legged iron pot and put some of every cow's milk in the pot also a pound of pins she hung the pot on the fire. As the pot began to boil on the fire the one that bewitched the milk from the cows stood outside the window crying and praying to the woman inside to take the pot off the fire that every pin in the pot was jagging her.

A solemn oath was exacted, and she never interfered with those cows again though Mrs Higginson hints that she continued to operate elsewhere. 'It was said that these witches could go into any shape but the shape of a hare was most favoured'; and it may or may not be significant that, even in my own time, the local people, though they used to buy quantities of rabbits from the keeper's department, would never take a hare under any circumstances whatever. It was almost as if they were afraid of eating their old aunt by accident.

The Evil Eye is attributed only to one woman in Mrs Higginson's record, a peculiar creature with a double set of bones in her chest. It was very unlucky to meet her when setting out on a journey, and the fishermen said that if they met her on the way to the fishing 'they would catch no fish that night'. Second sight, of course, was harmless. It was possessed in particular by a poetess called Janet Grahame, who foretold, among other things, the ruin of the Fraser family. She was 'well educated both in Gaelic and English she could preach a sermon or give a lecture as well as many a minister. She could compose a song in a few minutes'.

Another loss which must have resulted from the rationalisation of the farms, and from the consequent great decrease in the population as a whole, was that of the 'all-round' men who could turn their hands to a variety of different jobs. Epitaphs such as that of the tailor at Caolfin, and Mrs Higginson's allusions to the shoemaker at Laggan and the joiner at Strone, point to the presence in the farming 'townships' of men who pursued some skilled trade when work for the farming tenant or tenants was slack. Something has already been said about the function of 'cottars' in the old agricultural system, together with the possible significance of the groups of houses marked at farm sites by Roy; and a certain number of tailors, shoemakers, wrights and weavers probably came into this category, to say nothing about pipers and persons lacking obvious means of support. There were also the farmers who fished and the fishermen who farmed, to borrow the definitions applied to Orcadians and Shetlanders respectively; and also owners of wherries and other kinds of craft, who together point to a considerable involvement with the sea. Mrs Higginson writes of wherries running to Portincross, in Ayrshire, with cargo or passengers, the fare being one shilling, and Mrs Campbell notes, in 1813, how 'the usual picturesque fleet of boats set out for Largs fair'. There was even a boatyard at Skipness, where, again in 1813, a new wherry for the laird was launched by one Duncan MacPhail; the yard must presumably have been in the tidal pool in the former mouth of the burn, where a photograph taken in 1877 shows four smacks and two large rowing-boats grounded at low tide, and where the last of the local fishermen, MacCallums and MacKinlays, persisted until the middle of the 1890s. I recall the high, pole-built staging beside the pool, on which they dried their nets. There can, I think, be no doubt that a community which contained such a number of varied elements must have had a spicier taste than its late-Victorian successor, in which everyone worked at some particular job, for the laird or a responsible farmer.

Not the least interesting feature of Georgian Skipness must have been the manufacture and export of illicit whisky. The furious denunciation of this 'unholy and unpatriotic traffic', delivered in 1843 by the minister of Kilcalmonell and Kilberry, has been quoted above on p.117, but his colleague in Saddell and Skipness, at the same date, adopted a much calmer tone. 'Smuggling', he says,

> which at one time was the chief employment of crofters and fishermen in winter, is now almost entirely suppressed and abandoned. The fierce and daring encounters of the Skipness men with the officers of the excise was long proverbial. It was no uncommon exploit with them to overpower a whole crew of cuttersmen, then to carry off their oars and tackle, and coolly set them adrift in their own boats.

Mrs Robert Campbell witnessed an affair of this kind in 1813, while sailing in the Revenue cutter from Greenock to Skipness, and records that

> Captain Robinson was rather anxious to kidnap some smugglers after whom he had sent his boats . . . His boat picked up a Skipness boat with 8 casks, but met with much resistance and much fighting, and left some of the smugglers with severe

wounds which will probably give *me* some doctoring when I go home.

One of the Hyndmans who lived at the Old Pier once gave my father an old rusty claymore which had been taken from a Revenue officer by one of the Skipness men in just such a sea-fight. The Campbells, living in what must have been the *blütezeit* of smuggling, were evidently as little put out by it as the minister of thirty years later, as Mrs Campbell records that her husband, who had meanwhile warned the people to hide their stills, brought the gauger, a Mr Mitchell, in to tea; and a fortnight later another, this time a Mr Nicol, was asked to dinner as the laird made 'a point of being civil to him on account of the villagers, and I believe he is a very good-natured gauger'. The shipping to Bute of a boatload of people and eight casks of whisky on a January night was mentioned above on p.12.

The villagers' point of view is presented by Mrs Higginson, who writes in part as follows:

> Many a hundred pound in Scots money was brought to the parish of Skipness from time immemorial . . . by whisky distillation many a hundred gallon left the parish that never smelled the gauger. Every farmer crofter and cottar was busy at the trade, the women were as capable as the men and many daring and narrow escapes they had, in many instances barely escaping from the officers by the skin of their teeth. They had their pot stills in every out of the way place where there was running water. There was always a watch kept on the sea for the approach of the Revenue cutter and on the hills for fear of the gaugers . . .

Security precautions, however, were not always effective, and the story was told of a woman who fled up Glen Skibble carrying the worm of her still, and with a gauger, perhaps not the good-natured Mr Nicol, in hot pursuit. She made her escape by jumping down a precipice into the chasm, where she fell into a deep pool and took no harm. The Ancient Monuments Commission has found and recorded the site of an illicit still about four hundred yards north of the former New Pier. Another good example once existed in a tributary of the Crow Glen burn, quite close to the village, but this has been demolished in the course of timber operations.

This chapter may fitly end with a story of crime and punishment recorded by Mrs Robert Campbell. A man, it appears, whose name has not come down, got drunk on Communion Sunday, and to wind up an exciting day invaded the back regions of the House and made improper proposals to the servants. Next morning he was duly brought up in front of the laird, who was of course a magistrate. The laird had large numbers of whippy little switches cut, and served them out to all the women and girls in the village; the man was then deprived of his underclothes, though his trousers were left him for decency, and he was made to run the gauntlet of the switches all along the street. He was never heard of again.

Index

Knapdale 10
knitting 57, 77, 106
Knox, John 49

Lagan Geoidh 6, 62, 99,
  101, 113
Lagvoulin (Redhouse) 14, 114;
  and see inns
Larachmor see burns, cup-
  marked stones, graves
Largs Fair 130
Leachd na Gall 49; and see
  graves
Loch Awe school of sculpture
  47
lochs
  Caolisport 15
  Crinne 113
  Fyne 1, 2, 4, 5, 9, 12, 31
  Loch na Machrach Moire
    5, 113
  Loch na Machrach Rige 5
  Loch an Eilein 113
  Lochan a' Chreimh 113
  Lochan Fraoich 113
  Loch Romain 113
  Loch an t'Saoir Carridh 114
  West Loch Tarbert 4, 5
Lords of the Isles 14, 34, 35,
  39, 115
Lowlands and Lowlanders 12,
  116, 118, 123

MacArthur, Donald, Session
  Clerk 48, 49
McColl, Mrs, tinker 19
MacDonald, Alistair, son of
  Coll Ciotach (Colkitto) 40
McDougalls of Lorn 35

McGugan, Captain 11
McKillop, Ann, alleged witch
  128
McKillop, Janet 128
MacKinlay family, fishermen
  130
MacKinlay, Margaret,
  shopkeeper 55
MacKinlay, Ronald, shoemaker
  55
MacLachlan, Rev. John 50
MacLachlan, Neil, factor 91
Maclean, 'Granny' 58
Maclean, Peter, factor to R.C.
  Graham 125
Maclean, Charles, brother
  of Peter, farmer, Eascairt,
  Latinist 125
MacLachlan, Malcolm, of
  Dunderawe 40
MacNaughton, Rev. Duncan 50
Magnus Barefoot 14
masons 62, 69
meals and menus
  breakfast 75
  lunch 78
  shooting lunch 106
  tea 79
  dinner 80
  wedding feast 127
Menteith, Mrs, wife of Skipness
  innkeeper 123
Menzies, Rev. John M. 50
middens and ashpits 56,
  83, 120
mills, mill houses, mill field see
  Skipness Mill, Gartavaigh
Monkswell House, London
  residence of Collier cousins
  103

names 88
Neolithic people 24
newspapers 80
Nicolaisen, Prof. W.F.H. 2, 4

Oakes, Mr C.A.M. xvii
occult phenomena 61, 66, 86,
    114, 119, 122–5, 127–9
O'Malley, Lady (Ann Bridge)
    88
O'Malley, Owen St Clair,
    later Sir Owen, the author's
    cousin xvi, 111

Paisley Abbey 35, 46
parishes:
    Claonaig 17, 50
    Craignish 48
    Kilcalmonell and Kilberry
        17, 48, 116–7, 130
    Saddell and Cardell 50
    Saddell and Killean 17
    Saddell and Skipness 17,
        50, 117
    Skipness, *quoad sacra* 50
paupers 116
picnics and sitting out of doors
    79, 99, 101
piers and landings:
    Altagalvash Bay 12, 199
    Brann a' Phuirt or Shell
        Bay 9, 10
    Brian Phort 12
    Fishery Board harbour 10
    Jetty 9
    New Pier 10, 119, 132
    Port a' Chruidh (Chro) 10
plague 116
ploughmen 47, 97

plumber 69
population 116, 118
Post Office and postal
    arrangements 11, 21–2,
    55–6, 79–80
potting sheds 8, 84, 87
prayers and services in the
    House 65, 75, 77
precentor 50
Presbyterianism 16, 48–50, 77

quarries 33, 46

rabbits 109
raised beach 3, 10, 33, 101
Ramsay, Prof. George, author's
    uncle 102
Rathlin 5
Rawlinson, Thomas 30
Redhouse 14
Rent Book 1836 52
rhododendrons 101
Robert Bruce, King of Scots
    14, 36
Robinson, Captain, Excise
    Officer 130
Roman Catholics 12, 16

Saint Columba 16, 58; *and see*
    chapels
Sandy Bay 93
schools
    Claonaig 50, 55
    Skipness 21, 53, 54, 55
    Sperasaig 55
Schuyler, Adoniah, Captain
    R.N., father of Susan
    qv, the author's great-
    grandfather xvii
Schuyler, Susan Roope, wife of

Detail of Ordnance Survey map of 1899, showing the Skipness House of 1881.